Praise for Therez Fleetwood and
The Afrocentric Bride

"Bridal Designer Therez Fleetwood marries African influences with haute couture for **a stunning take on wedding gowns.**"
> —**Essence** magazine

"**Therez Fleetwood has the creative vision, ability and skill to combine traditional African design elements with contemporary styling to design exciting, elegant and regal gowns** for brides who choose to reflect their cultural heritage in their wedding gowns. **This book is a must read!**"
> —**Harriette Cole, President & Creative Director, Profundities, Inc.; Author of**
> ***Jumping the Broom***

"**Looking for a gown that expresses your heritage?** Therez Fleetwood creates unique dresses with African inspirations. Her design style can be described as "**ethnic elegance**.""
> —**The Knot**

"Afrocentric design has 'come of age' with Therez Fleetwood's timeless and creative flair, offering today's modern bride **an authentic taste of African style and sophistication**".
> —**Bola Obileye, Publisher, *Continental Bride***

"**As a former winner of the Linden New Day Designer's Competition**, as one of the nation's leading bridal designer's **and as a nationally renowned author, Therez Fleetwood never ceases to amaze me.**"
> —**John Blassingame, Publisher, *Today's Black Woman*;**
> **President, Linden New Day Associates**

With inspired **African flair and splendor**, Therez Fleetwood presents **bridal elegance and gorgeous gowns with style.** This is required, **MUST READING**, to help you design your very own, picture-perfect successful wedding day.
> —**Alfred Fornay, Author of *The African-American Woman's Guide to***
> ***Successful Make-up and Skin Care* and *Born Beautiful: The***
> ***African-American Teenager's Complete Beauty Guide*; Publisher and**
> **Editor-in-Chief, *Luxe Living Magazine***

"I have to find a husband just so I can get that dress on the cover and have a reason to wear it. **It is beyond gorgeous!** I love the book!"
> —**Milca Esdaille, *Quarterly Black Review***

More Praise For Therez Fleetwood and The Afrocentric Bride

"Therez, I LOVE your designs! **My husband and I were very pleased with my dress.** Wishing you continued success. I take pride in saying I got married wearing a Therez Fleetwood."
   —**Tamara (Leftridge) Whitehurst**

"Therez's design for my wedding dress was gorgeous. **I truly felt like an African queen.**"
   —**Lysa (Hendrick) Straughter**

"Therez and her team were a pleasure to work with. They provided **an excellent service.**"
   —**Sara Voylas**

"My Fairy God Mother, **without your magical touch, I would have been just another bride.** Thank you so much for making me feel and look like an African Queen. Wishing you the most success and happiness. You deserve it!
   —**Shannell Kwantu**

"You have made my wedding truly a day to remember. All my guests could not stop commenting on **how beautiful my dress was.**"
   —**Jennifer Ortiz**

"Hat's off to a consummate professional! Therez has married **refined elegance with a design touch all her own.** Her use of intricate needlework to the simplicity of her beaded designs are only two of the ways she has managed to set herself apart from other bridal designers. It was a joy to collaborate with someone so passionate about her work."
   —**Monique Sulle Brown**

"Every bride wants to look beautiful on her wedding day. **Knowing that I was wearing a Therez Fleetwood creation** made me feel like a Nubian Princess. (90% of our guests thought I was one.) My husband, however, thought I was a true African Queen."
   —**Betsey E. Jackson**

The Afrocentric Bride
A Style Guide

The Afrocentric Bride
A Style Guide

Therez Fleetwood

Amber Books

Phoenix
New York   Los Angeles

The Afrocentric Bride: A Style Guide

by Therez Fleetwood

Published by:
Amber Books
A Division of Amber Communication Group, Inc.
1334 East Chandler Boulevard, Suite 5-D67
Phoenix, AZ 85048
amberbk@aol.com
www.amberbooks.com

Tony Rose, Publisher/Editorial Director
Yvonne Rose, Senior Editor

Samuel P. Peabody, Associate Publisher
The Printed Page, Interior & Cover Design

The publication is designed to provide accurate and authoritative information in regard to the subject matter covered. It is sold with the understanding that the Publisher is not engaged in rendering legal, accounting or other professional services. If legal advice or other expert assistance is required, the services of a competent professional person should be sought.

AMBER BOOKS are available at special discounts for bulk purchases, sales promotions, fund raising or educational purposes.

Library of Congress Cataloging-In-Publication Data

Fleetwood, Therez.
  The Afrocentric bride : a style guide / Therez Fleetwood.
    p. cm.
  ISBN 0-9727519-1-2
  1. Wedding costume--United States. 2. African Americans--Marriage customs and rites. 3. Weddings--United States--Planning. I. Title.
  GT1753.U6 .F54 2003
  392.5'089'96073--dc21

                    2003042640

Dedication

A beautiful woman once told me to
"reach for the moon and I'll fall amongst the stars"
—I've never forgotten that.

Thanks Mom, I love you.

Acknowledgments

In life we must have passion in order to move ahead and achieve greatness. I am so very fortunate to have discovered my passion and am able to share it with the rest of the world.

I'd like to give thanks and acknowledgment to the following people who have made my journey a joyous one.

Tony Rose, what can I say to the man who never lets me forget how great I am. I love you 'Dad'.

Yvonne Rose, my Mom, who bought me my first sewing machine at the age of 12, and who's love and support has guided me thus far.

Kevin Fleetwood, my big 'bro', you always keep me laughing when times get hard.

Valerie, **Jalessa** and **Zahara**, just know that all things are possible.

Shawn Rhea, **Camille Ward** and **Robin Credle**: What would I do without friends like you in my life? You always give me the strength to keep moving forward.

Henry Rock: Thank you for supporting me since day one.

Miriam Muley, Surprise! You always saw the best in me, thank you!

Franklin Rowe, **Cassandra Bromfield**, **Sherrie Hobson-Greene**, **Brian Osborne** and **Johnathen Adewami**, I'm so fortunate to have friends like you.

Grege, **Nicki**, **Dionne** and **Veroy**, you girls are beautiful inside and out.

Harriette Cole, you inspired me to design my first Afrocentric wedding gown.

Carley Roney, who launched my bridal collection along with her website, www.theknot.com, and has believed in me ever since.

And lastly, my deepest gratitude to my clients. Without your support, this book would not be possible.

Therez Fleetwood

...and to our dear friend, Carole Hall, whose respect and friendship for Amber Books helps make us better publishers, always.
—Tony Rose, Publisher & CEO, Amber Books and
  Yvonne Rose, Senior Editor & VP, Amber Books

Contents

About the Author

Therez Fleetwood, who attended the Fashion Institute of Technology (F.I.T.) in New York, began her career in Ethnic design with the launching of her Phe-Zula Collection. It was a well received line of casual, career and formal attire often featured in *Elle, Italian Glamour, Women's Wear Daily*, and *The New York Times*. Phe-Zula's clients included Angela Bassett, Vanessa Williams, Queen Latifah and the popular recording group En Vogue, who she dressed for the 1991 Grammy Awards.

After Ms. Fleetwood was asked to design a wedding dress exclusively for *Jumping the Broom* by Harriette Cole, she launced the Therez Fleetwood Bridal Collection. Her nationally acclaimed Ethnic bridal gowns began to appear in magazines such as *In Style Weddings, Essence, Signature Bride*, and *Black Elegance*. She designed the only wedding gown to be featured in the *Essence By Mail* catalogue and was one of 35 designers to have a display in the "New York Gets Married" exhibit at the Museum of the City, May-September, 1997.

The Therez Fleetwood Bridal Collection was chosen for the American Express national commercial entitled "Portraits" and shortly thereafter Ms. Fleetwood appeared on the *NBC Today Show*. Among her many accolades, Ms. Fleetwood was named "The New Day Designer of the Year," was selected as one of the New York Museum's top designers for their "New York Gets Married" exhibit, and has earned the Allstate Insurance Company's "From Whence We Came: African-American Women of Triumph" Award.

Foreword

There was a time not so long ago when brides felt confined to the strict wedding rules set before them, when weddings were carbon-copy celebrations almost completely devoid of personal touches, and when bridal gowns all looked the same. Then along came Therez Fleetwood who took a chance and broke the modern wedding gown mold.

I have a strong admiration for forward-thinking pioneers in the bridal industry, and Ms. Fleetwood is one of the most remarkable women I've come to know in the wedding world. For so long, ethnic-American women dreamed of dresses that were infused with culture and complexity, of gowns that would make a statement about who these women were and convey something of their history on their special days. And just when it seemed that the fashion world wasn't ready to fulfill what they were looking for, Ms. Fleetwood filled the void and unveiled a dramatic, beautiful collection of gowns just for these special brides.

She has the amazing ability to merge exquisite details and gorgeous fabrics—from Nigerian Aso-oke cloth to Guinea brocade—with ethnically and regionally influenced designs. Because her inspiration spans the globe from northern Africa to India to the Caribbean, there is a piece of her cultural affection woven into every gown she creates.

Ms. Fleetwood is a woman who is not afraid to take chances, who is not afraid to move against the trends, and who is not afraid to express her fashion sensibilities, both culturally and esthetically. Celebrities love her. Brides love her. And the wedding industry loves her too. She has done us all a great service by being true to who she is—and true to the women she represents.

Carley Roney
The Knot (www.theknot.com)
Cofounder & Editor in Chief

Throughout my travels in Western and Southern Africa,
I was always in awe of the jewelry, sculpture and artwork
in the different countries. Designing ethnic wedding gowns
is my passion and when a bride comes into my studio proclaiming
"Thank God I found you; you understand what I'm looking for!
I know that I am blessed."

—Therez Fleetwood

Introduction

I have always been interested in fashion, art and design. At the age of twelve I began designing clothes and by age fifteen, I was entering and winning designer competitions back in my hometown of Boston, Massachusetts.

As I grew older, I became intrigued by the bright, colorful patterns often used in African fabrics and began creating garments from these exotic prints. Being an African-American woman, I wanted to create a sophisticated collection of ethnic clothing reflective of my personality, lifestyle and heritage. My designs were not cut in the traditional silhouettes worn throughout Africa, but rather trendy silhouettes worn throughout America. It was important to me to incorporate both of these cultures in a way that reflected my personal fashion statement.

I became known worldwide for my fashion-forward ethnic designs—form-fitted bustier dresses, hip-hugging bell-bottom pants and exotic evening wear—all made out of exotic prints. As my collection grew, my celebrity clientele increased. My fashions were viewed on several network television programs and featured in a variety of national and international publications. Harriette Cole, the Fashion Editor of *Essence* magazine, first inspired me to design bridal wear, when she asked me to create an Afrocentric wedding dress exclusively for her book *Jumping the Broom, The African-American Wedding Planner*. The design direction of the bridal gown, which incorporated different

fabrications with hand-beading and gold embroidered trims, was so unique that requests for it came pouring in.

More and more African-American brides and grooms were choosing to express their ethnicity through their choice of wedding styles. I researched the market and discovered that not many companies were catering to the Afrocentric wedding niche; and decided to devote my design expertise to creating a collection of wedding dresses that would offer the African-American bride something special. After all, this day will be one of the most memorable and cherished days of your life. You've found your perfect man; and now the search begins for your perfect dress. The gown you choose should bolster your confidence and reflect your personal style.

Whether you plan to have an authentically African or vaguely Afrocentric wedding, this book will help you choose wedding attire that will enhance your figure and delight you totally. Afrocentric bridal attire does not fall under just one category. As an African-American bride, you have more choices then ever in selecting a wedding gown that reflects your style and heritage, as you will see throughout this book. Traditional African wedding attire requires wrapping fabric around the body, which creates flattering unconstructed silhouettes. Whereas, contemporary silhouettes can use the same African fabrics cut, shaped, seamed and darted to enhance a bride's figure.

I was motivated to write *The Afrocentric Bride* because of my desire to offer African-American brides cultural choices in selecting their wedding attire. *I was inspired* to write this book because of my clients. Through their tears and laughter, we planned and produced their dream-wedding look. My clients do not always know exactly what they are looking for when searching for an Afrocentric wedding dress; but they know that they want to wear something cultural and reflective of their personality.

As our consciousness of our heritage is displayed through music, art dance and fashion, we are seeking more ways to incorporate this awareness into other aspects of our lives. We, as a people are so unique in our individuality—and making a personal statement with our wedding attire is a reflection of who we are. For many brides, Afrocentric styles are the perfect choice, because they combine contemporary European and American silhouettes and images with African elements. *The Afrocentric Bride—A Style Guide* was written to provide African-American brides with answers to *all* your questions regarding wedding styles for your *perfect wedding day.*

Therez Fleetwood

Chapter 1
Choosing Your Wedding Style

You've waited a lifetime for this special day; and finally, it's time to create the most beautiful vision of yourself on one of the happiest days of your life. But, now confusion sets in, as you are deciding what style direction you want to take. Selecting your dress is a big decision that has more to do with just how you look on that day; it is the ultimate expression of your personal style.

The choice of your Afrocentric wedding gown will impact almost every other aspect of your wedding, transcending far beyond how you look gliding down the aisle. It will set the tone for the rest of the ceremony and influence other details of your perfect wedding. The style of your wedding gown also helps to determine the level of formality and affects what everyone else in the wedding party will be wearing.

Every bride has a different vision of herself and the kind of dress she wants to wear on her wedding day. Whatever style you choose is a matter of personal taste. As an *Afrocentric* bride your choices are not limited. First, you and your fiancé' should decide whether you want a formal, semiformal or informal wedding. Then, before you select your dress, consider what elements of African culture you want to incorporate into your ceremony and think about what region of Africa you would like to take those elements from.

In wedding planning, your gown is the centerpiece. Basically, everything else is built around it. The gown sets the style and formality for the ceremony and reception.

For example, you might wish to try Egyptian inspired fashions that combine hieroglyphics and draped silhouettes, which have been designed with Kings and Queens in mind. For an elegant accent, take the time to research beautifully carved gold jewelry and regal fabrics such as hand woven Aso-oke or Kente cloth from West Africa. You'd make a beautiful fashion statement by mixing satins, silks or brocade fabrics with Turag crosses, silver trinkets and chiffon veils reminiscent of North African styles. You could apply a myriad of colorful beaded patterns like those that are used to adorn the garments and reflect the culture in Southern Africa. Or, maybe you would prefer to choose East Africa influences by using decorative ornaments of metals, wood, glass and shells to enhance a contemporary wedding gown.

When defining your wedding style and the type of wedding you want to have, you must ask yourself the following questions:

1. *Where are we getting married? In a church? On a beach? At home?*

   To determine the formality of your wedding, this is usually the first question that you and your fiancé ask. Once you agree on this, you can begin to shape the rest of your ceremony.

2. *How do I see myself walking down the aisle on my big day?*

   What you choose to wear is determined by the formality and authenticity of your wedding. The cultural influences you choose to incorporate into your wedding attire are best determined by how elegant, romantic, sexy, or modern you would like to be.

3. *How culturally authentic would we like our wedding to be?*

   You can choose to have touches of African culture throughout your ceremony and your attire by mixing African elements with European traditions. Or, you may choose to have a full-blown authentic African ceremony, wearing traditional attire and a being led by drum precession.

4. *What type of wedding dress will fit my personality and reflect the style of the wedding that my fiancé and I are choosing to have?*

By now you should have an idea of the type of bridal gown that will reflect your personal style and create a signature statement for your wedding. Next, visualize the style that you will be most comfortable in and make a decision about what region of Africa will best suit your needs.

5. *How large will the wedding party be?*

The size of your wedding party will be determined by the formality of your wedding. Formal weddings can have as many as ten attendants for both the bride and the groom. Whereas informal weddings can have only one.

6. *How will we incorporate the theme into the bridal parties' wardrobe?*

Your bridal gown should create a signature statement for your wedding. As an African-American bride, you should select a dress that makes you feel the royalty of your ancestry, placing a tangible reality toward the concept of "African Queen."

Once you determine your style and the regional African influences you want to incorporate into your wedding dress, selecting the wardrobe for your bridal party will be a whole lot easier. If you've chosen to wear traditional African garments or more contemporary fabrics using African motifs, then the bridal party's wardrobe should reflect that which you are wearing.

Now, you must determine what bridal style you are most comfortable wearing. Do you prefer contemporary, alternative, traditional or heirloom? A contemporary bride often wants to wear a Western style silhouette and adds touches of Afrocentric elements to her dress. An alternative bride prefers smart, sexy styles, either cut from ethnic fabrics or accented with trims, such as cowrie shells, Ethiopian crosses, African beads or embroidery. A traditional bride enjoys an authentic African look from the Motherland made from a beautiful hand-woven fabrics like Aso-oke or Kente cloth fabric. An heirloom bride takes pride in her roots and wants to wear a dress passed down within her family.

Chapter 2
The Contemporary Bride

Contemporary Afrocentric bridal attire is a mixture of African elements combined with European silhouettes. The selection is quite vast, including:

- ❋ Body-hugging silhouettes

- ❋ Empire styles

- ❋ Sheaths, ballgowns and A-lines accented with deep plunging necklines

- ❋ Sexy front and side slits

- ❋ Trumpet hemlines and fishtail extensions.

The most popular fabrics used to create these fashion forward styles are silk, satin, chiffon and organza, adorned with specific trims that give your dress a contemporary feel.

My company, the Therez Fleetwood Bridal Collection, specializes in Contemporary Afrocentric wedding gowns. When I design a wedding dress, I think about brides who are like me—fashion-forward African-American women who want to wear figure-flattering dresses that incorporate subtle hints of our African culture.

As a contemporary bride, you may choose to reveal your artistic expression by adorning your wedding dress with colorful beadwork created by the Ndbele and Maasai peoples of South

You'll want to look and feel truly radiant on your perfect wedding day. All eyes are on you as you glide down the aisle, so choose a dress they won't soon forget.

Sisters are so beautiful!

Africa. You might even opt to wear a form-fitted sheath with gold embroidered trim and silk satin fabric accented by hiero-glyphics and gold beads, making you feel like an Egyptian royalty. Or you may want to look and feel like the ultimate princess on your wedding day, by wearing an A-line silhouette with a fitted bodice accented by pearlized cowrie shells and tiny pearls and detachable train.

A Bride's Story

Monique, a six-foot tall beauty with a size 18 frame, was voluptuous with a thick waistline. Therefore, the gown she chose had to draw attention away from her waist and create a slimming silhouette. It was also very important to her to select a Contemporary style with African elements to pay homage to her father and her Ghanaian ancestry. She chose a three-piece wedding dress that was a bustier top and halter back. I hand-stitched over 500 cowrie shells onto her top, which gave an ethnic element to her over-all look. She wore an A-line skirt, made of silk shantung and a chapel length train that detached after the ceremony, so that she could move with ease throughout the reception.

Chapter 3
The Alternative Bride

Traditionally, ballgowns and A-line shapes have been the most universal silhouettes in wedding gowns. However, this is no longer the case. Today, there are more options then ever in choosing your wedding attire. Because, there are no set rules, more and more African-American women are selecting Alternative styles for their wedding dresses, designed in various colors, lengths and shapes.

There are a growing number of African-American brides choosing Alternative wedding dresses. I have found that most of my clients who choose to wear Alternative wedding dresses are having small ceremonies with a limited guest list of immediate family members and close friends. They fall into the category of either mature; getting married for the second time around; or they simply want a dress they can wear after the wedding.

Brides can be influenced by several factors when choosing to wear an alternative wedding dress.

If you prefer the Alternative styles, you can select an evening gown, cocktail dress or even a suit, made from African fabrics like Aso-oke or guinea brocade. Perhaps you might choose a simple, solid colored silk dress accessorized with a gele (head-wrap) and shawl. Or, you may prefer to wear elaborate jewelry inspired by North African culture, such as Turag crosses, made of metal, that symbolize luck, protection and power, mixed with variously shaped beads of amber, coral or glass.

Your personal statement is what's important and your bridal attire should reflect that. So, choose a style that is right for you—one that flatters your figure, is comfortable to wear, and makes you feel awesome.

A Bride's Story

Shannell came to me with a vision that she wanted to float down the aisle in the colors of the South African sunset. She was greatly influenced by the Zulu culture and wanted to incorporate this into her wedding attire. With this in mind, I designed an overcoat made from 7 yards of silk chiffon fabric, which was tie-dyed in graduating hues of orange and gold and accented with embroidered trim and gold hand-painted cowrie shells. Underneath she wore a form-fitted bustier dress with an exaggerated trumpet hemline, in a deep gold silk charmeuse fabric with a tint of orange contrast that accented her curvaceous figure. To top off Shannell's ensemble, I created a beaded necklace, inspired by the Maasai peoples of Southern Africa, designed to resemble the beautiful beadwork from this region.

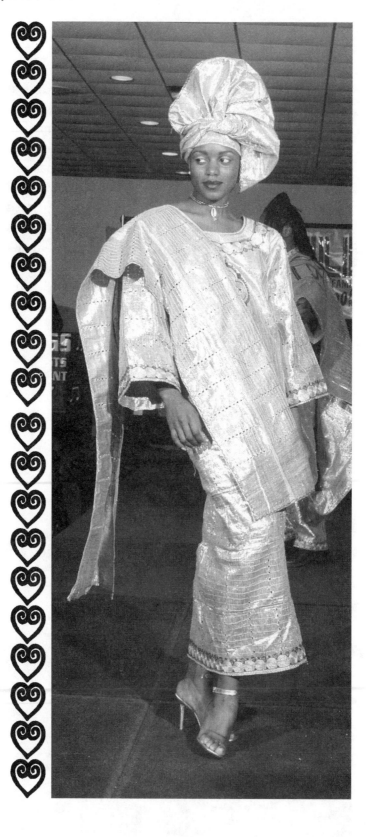

Chapter 4
The Traditional Bride

Wearing traditional African bridal attire is an excellent way to make a truly authentic and visual statement. However, there are several styles and silhouettes that can represent the authenticity of the attire you choose depending on the country in Africa you would like to represent. Just, imagine the array of style possibilities that represent the 53 African countries. The most commonly defined traditional wedding attire is that from West Africa, which consists of a "buba" or blouse, an "iro" or body wrap, an "iborun" or shawl, and a "gele" or head-tie. All of the pieces are made of colorful hand-woven fabrics.

The traditional silhouettes look great on all shapes and sizes. Whether your stature is short and round, or tall and slender you can wrap the skirt tightly around your body and mid-section and the blouse will be full enough to camouflage or accentuate your waistline. The beauty of the "wrap" is that no matter what size you wear, your garment will still look good because you are not confined to the contours of a fitted gown.

When wearing traditional garb, there are no rules about color. Colors have meaning only to the extent of expressing what you want to symbolize, or just for elaborating or enriching your wedding theme.

The most common types of fabrics used in traditional African bridal styles are aso-oke, george, brocade, kente, and jacquard. Oftentimes, these fabrics are adorned with silver or gold embroidery stitched throughout the garment and decorated with Adinkra symbols that represent unity, strength, and spiritual principles. Embroidered patterns are also created with Egyptian hieroglyphics, the most popular being the "Ankh," the sign of life.

The most popular traditional African styles are as follows:

Kaba Set   Lace peplum top with straight kente skirt.

Mameboye   Dress and head-wrap of matching print worn with lots of jewelry.

Tabas   Peplum top with leg-of-mutton sleeves and straight skirt.

Bubah   Consists of 4 pieces; the shirt (buba), the wrap (Iro), the headwrap (gele), and shawl (iborun). Usually made out of kente cloth fabric in any color expressly chosen for the bride and worn with elaborate jewelry.

A Designer's Story

According to Jonathan Adewami of Nigerian Fabrics and Fashions, "In West Africa alone, you have a situation where there are hundreds of dialects, and that would be hundreds of different cultures, and in those cultures you can even have a further breakdown of what they would classify as their wedding attire. Each culture has a different ceremony, different attire and different fabrics that would be used."

Chapter 5
The Heirloom Bride

Wearing an heirloom gown that has been handed down from your mother, grandmother or close friend, is one of the oldest traditions in America and can be very sentimental and meaningful. For African-American brides who want a Southern feel to their wedding, an heirloom gown can provide the perfect combination of family tradition and personal expression.

With a good tailor or seamstress, it is very easy to rework an heirloom gown and create your desired look. As an option, if the heirloom gown cannot be altered to fit, you can wear part of it by removing the sections that do not fit or are damaged, and work with the remaining pieces. For best results, ask a dressmaker to advise you of your options. This can help you decide which parts of the gown you want to have modified or simplified. Some simple styling solutions could involve shortening or removing the sleeves, altering the hemline or contouring the bodice.

For your own unique style, beautiful patchworks can be created by using various types of silk fabrics and pieces from a few heirloom dresses to give your gown a truly authentically Southern feel. However, if you want to create a patchwork fabric, make sure the seamstress altering your dress is familiar with this process. It is best to create the fabric first; and then cut your pattern pieces according to your desired results.

> By adding specific adornments to parts of the dress, you'll be able to incorporate an Afrocentric theme.

George, kente, rabal cloth or other African fabrics can be applied along certain sections of the dress, such as the hemline or bodice; or you may prefer to use cowrie shells, beads or ethnic trinkets.

Regardless of your choice, be sure to check the strength of the fabric before applying any adornments because some fabrics do breakdown over a certain amount of time and could tear easily.

To create a more contemporary feel, you might wish to add tulle, embellished with hand-painted Adinkra symbols, on the skirt and train of the gown.

You can also add a nice touch to an heirloom dress by creating a decorative beadwork pattern and applying it along the neckline, bodice and/or sleeves. So, if it is your decision to be an heirloom bride, give yourself plenty of time to make alterations or embellishments to your dress.

A Designer's Story

Bridal designer Cassandra Bromfield pulls specifically from your family history in order to create your wedding dress. For example, she will dig into your mother's bureau for a special antique handkerchief and incorporate it into your gown. "In many ways, something that's really important to the bride, like her grandmother's handkerchief, might be just as Afrocentric as putting a cowrie shell on her dress," says Bromfield.

Chapter 6
Formal, Semi-Formal or Informal?

There are three categories of weddings: formal, semiformal and informal. The formality is determined by the location of the ceremony and reception, the size of the wedding party, the number of guests and the time of day.

Once you've decided on the time of day and location of your wedding, make sure the gown you choose is appropriate to this setting. For example, you wouldn't want to wear the same type of dress for a formal evening wedding as you might wear at an informal afternoon wedding. A Saturday night wedding traditionally warrants a more formal gown than a Sunday afternoon wedding.

Sometimes, by working various elements of a formal wedding into an informal one, you can make a less formal wedding elegant and sophisticated.

> It could be appropriate to wear a shorter gown for a Saturday night wedding.

I've included some specifics to help you understand the style choices associated with your perfect wedding.

Formal Weddings

❊ The ceremony usually takes place in a house of worship, a large home or garden.

❊ The bride and her attendants (usually from 4 to 10 bridesmaids) wear long gowns.

❋ The bridal gown should be elegant and flowing. A long dress with a chapel, sweep or detachable train would be worn for a formal wedding. Rich fabrics are used, such as satin, silk, lace, brocade, velvet, aso-oke and george; either in white, ivory, pastels, gold or silver colors. You would carry a full bouquet.

❋ Details like gloves and an elegant headpiece are added to increase the formality.

❋ Veils are usually shoulder, fingertip, chapel or cathedral lengths.

❋ Bridesmaids would wear long dresses, with complementary hair ornaments. They can carry any style bouquet.

❋ The groom and his attendants (usually from 4 to 10 ushers) wear cutaways or tailcoats.

❋ The Groom and his ushers would wear a cutaway jacket, a waistcoat with matching trousers or a tuxedo; a wing-collar shirt and a bow tie and cummerbund; or a dress shirt with an ascot and vest. Summer options include white or off white dinner jackets and dark pants.

❋ The formal reception is usually a sit-down or semi-buffet meal.

❋ Music (if the reception includes dancing) is often provide by a full band.

Semi-Formal Weddings

❋ The ceremony can take place in a house of worship, chapel, hotel, club, home or garden.

❋ The bride and her attendants (usually 2 to 6 brides-maids) may wear tea-length gowns usually made of simpler fabrics then those for a formal wedding.

❋ Bridal gowns range from floor-length to above the knee and can be worn with a splash of color and coordinating headpiece and/or veil. The most popular colors are white, ivory and various pastels; even gold and silver are appropriate. Fabrics such as silk, satin, aso-oke, kente and brocade work best.

❋ Veils can be shoulder, fingertip, chapel, waltz or ballet lengths.

❋ The bridesmaid dresses can range from floor-length to just above the knee. They can all be different colors and different silhouettes.

❋ The groom and his attendants (usually 2 to 6 ushers). A formal suit in a choice of colors and styles, a white or colored shirt, necktie, bow tie or ascot and vest. or a dinner jacket and trousers with a dress shirt and tie. He can opt to wear a monochromatic look, for his overall ensemble, with his shirt, tie, jacket and pants all made out of the same color. Or he can wear a nehru or mandarin styled jacket with matching pants and band collar shirt.

❋ The reception is generally a buffet or cocktail buffet.

❋ The music is typically provided by a small band or deejay.

Informal Weddings

✺ The ceremony for a casual or informal wedding usually takes place in a house of worship, chapel or rectory, outside on a beach, in a tent, a family member's home, the backyard where you grew up or perhaps in the "Islands".

✺ The bride and her attendants (usually 1 to 3 bridesmaids) have the widest range of selections for gowns.

✺ You can wear an elegant evening or cocktail dress, a two-piece suit or a simple wedding dress designed with your choice of hemlines. Although some informal gowns might have a slight "brush" train, which slightly sweeps the floor, most have no train at all. All color choices are acceptable, including: white, ivory, pastels, and jewel tones, using a fabric such as silk, cotton, brocade or kente.

✺ Usually a hat or headpiece is worn without a veil. However, if you prefer to wear one, the appropriate length would be flyaway or elbow.

✺ Bridesmaids dresses are just as informal as the bride's. They can wear a variety of dresses or suits in numerous lengths, colors, and fabrications.

The daring Nubian bride!

✺ The groom and his attendants (usually 1 to 3 ushers) wear dark suits, or sports jackets or blazers with coordinating dress slacks, dress shirts and four-in-hand ties. They can also choose to wear oversized tunic shirts (falling about 4" above the knee), embroidered vests and drawstring trousers.

✺ The reception often takes place at the wedding site directly following the ceremony, in a restaurant, or at home with a caterer.

✺ Music can be provided by a single musician, a deejay or background tapes.

If an island wedding is your preference, the wedding gown you choose should be informal and easy to wear.

Island Weddings

Island weddings can provide a very romantic beginning for your marriage. White sand beaches, turquoise-colored waters, exotic flowers and gentle trade winds seem more than perfect for daytime weddings; whereas, moonlight soft steel-band music and scents of lush tropical foliage offer enchanting nights for lovers.

In addition to the colorful and romantic tapestry of the Caribbean, African-American couples are being drawn to the islands for their perfect wedding. It may be your second wedding and an intimate wedding service may be just right for you. A home-based wedding (large or small) might feel overwhelming because there are too many family members and friends, which makes the task of setting a realistic guest list impossible.

If an island wedding is your preference, the wedding gown you choose should be informal and easy to wear.

Chapter 7

The Anatomy of Your Wedding Dress

Most brides have an idea of the type of wedding gown they are looking for, however finding the right dress is no easy task. The most important thing to consider is that the silhouette you choose is figure flattering and comfortable to wear. Your gown can be a simple sheath that you step into and zip up the back with ease, or it can have complicated closures, stiff lining and full skirt and train, which will require assistance from your designer or bridal attendant.

Arlete, a single mother of two was marrying for the second time. She had a voluptuous shape and a thick waistline. She wanted a silhouette that would draw attention away from her waist and have a slimming effect. It was important to her to pay homage to her ancestry by wearing a wedding dress that had cultural accents. She chose a 3-piece wedding dress that had a form-fitting bustier top with a peplum hemline. The peplum was cut an additional 2" longer then the actual sample to further accent her waist and create a slimming effect for her hips.

Don't be Afraid to Experiment

Try different silhouettes to find the styles that look best on you. Keep an open mind. For example, maybe you never thought of wearing something off the shoulder or in a sheath style until now.

She wore a long fitted skirt, tailored to her hips, which fell straight down to the hemline. Her train was a chapel length, A-line shape with a front opening. The edges of the bustier top and train were completely trimmed in natural cowrie shells.

Once you determine your style, then you must determine how
you want your dress to look. Answering the following questions will help you select the appropriate style of your wedding
gown.

What silhouette will best flatter your body type?

Take a look at your body, form head to toe, to determine its shape. Are your shoulders broad, your hips narrow, or is your bustline large? Whatever your shape, there are gown styles that you can choose to complement your overall appearance.

What kind of silhouette would you prefer? (ballgown, A-line, empire waist, straight sheath, a body-conscious style or a chic, modern suit?)

The silhouette you choose will also be determined by the formality of your wedding, (as was discussed in Chapter 6). Once you have an idea of the dress shape you want to wear, you can further enhance your look with the neckline, sleeve, bodice and length that you choose.

What dress length are you most comfortable wearing? (a floor length that grazes the top of the foot, tea length that extends down to the ankles, knee length or shorter?)

The dress length you choose will also depend on the type of wedding you are planning to have. Once you determine the hemline style for your dress, it will then be easier to determine the length.

Do you plan to wear a train?

Trains are optional. However, if you choose to wear one, it can be detachable, connecting at your shoulder or your waist. Or it can be an extension of your hemline.

The Fit and the Feel

Good fit and construction are absolutely essential.

☀ As you try on various wedding gowns, you'll notice that they have a different "feel" from ready to wear clothes. Wedding gowns may employ stays, boning wire, and stiff linings for contour and shape. Bodices can have complicated closures; and depending on the fabric and decorative applications, they can be heavy and constricting.

☀ If you choose to wear a contemporary ballgown or a full A-line dress, a petticoat or hoop skirt should be worn underneath to create fullness and shape. You may even have to practice walking before you feel graceful moving in these billowing skirts.

☀ Move around in your dress to make sure you can get in and out of limousines; kneel, bend and climb stairs. Raise your arms to make sure you have enough lift in your sleeves to throw the bouquet!

☀ A poorly constructed or ill-fitting garment could be a disaster on your wedding day, so make sure you have experienced hands working on your dress.

Are there aspects of your body that you want to accentuate or de-accentuate?

Some women have areas of their body that they want to either cover-up or show-off. Keep this in mind when selecting your dress. I've had many brides walk out of my studio with wedding gowns that push them up, pull them in and even give them curves.

Do you prefer stiff fabrics that contour your body or fabrics that are soft and relaxed?

The stiffer the fabric, the more you can tailor the dress to your figure and camouflage bulges. The softer the fabric, the more revealing it will be as it drapes your body.

What color will look best on your complexion?

Choosing the right color is very important. The wrong color will make your skin look sallow and dull, whereas, the right color will give your skin a healthy, radiant glow.

Do you want to adorn you dress with ethnic trims or African fabric?

How you envision yourself on your wedding day is very personal; and how you choose to express this vision will take some thought. Whether you choose ethnic trims or African fabric will depend on your level of comfort and how it fits with the overall theme of your wedding.

Shopping for your Afrocentric wedding gown can be both exhilarating and emotional. To find the best store or designer for your personal needs, take time to research. Read magazines, look online, ask friends, go to fashion shows and visit your local mall. A professional, trusted designer or salon can tell you what styles look best on you and give you the personal attention that you need to plan your perfect Afrocentric wedding.

Chapter 8
Dress Silhouettes

These are general guidelines to help you choose a dress that will complement your figure and make you feel comfortable all day on your wedding day.

The Empire

This is a fitted bodice with a high waistline that gathers right below the bustline and flares out into a graceful skirt.

A wedding dress on a hanger looks completely different than it does on a body. Choose several different silhouettes that you love and try them all on. If one brings tears to your eyes it is probably the right choice.

The Sheath

This is probably the most contemporary bridal gown look. A long column of fabric nipped at the waist, gives you a modern sleek look.

The Ballgown

This silhouette is timeless. It is the most traditional silhouette in the bridal industry. Made with clean lines, a fitted bodice, tapered waist and flowing skirt (or full-skirted) the ballgown often requires a crinoline, a full skirt made of tulle or boning worn under the dress to create a dramatic pouf. This style is the most romantic and flatters most body types.

The A-Line/Princess Style Dress

This is the most popular design for wedding dresses because it is flattering and fits many body types. It has vertical seams flowing from the armholes, over the bust, continuing to the hemline; and then it flares out creating an 'A' shape. The long line gives an illusion of an hourglass figure, making you look taller.

Traditional African Attire

This consists of an ankle-length wrap skirt, an unconstructed blouse and a shawl with a matching gele or headwrap. Because of the layering and wrapping effects of traditional African attire, your body shape is beautifully camouflaged.

Chapter 9
Putting It All Together

Lengths

The length you wear will depend on the formality of your wedding and your gown's silhouette. It can either add the illusion of height or make you appear shorter.

Floor	The longest hemline falls ½" from the floor, slightly brushing the floor (formal or semi-formal)
Ankle	The long hemline barely revels the ankles (formal or semi-formal)
Tea	This hemline falls several inches above the ankles (semi-formal or informal)
Knee	The short skirt falls just below the knee (informal)
Mini	The shortest skirt falls mid-thigh (informal)

Make sure the length you choose flatters your figure and is easy to move around in.

Hemlines

Hemlines add definition to the overall look of your dress. The right hemlines can work wonders in enhancing the shape of your hips; and they camouflage "saddle-bags". They can make a straight boyish figure sexy; or they can create a beautiful balance to your overall appearance. Here's a selection commonly used in bridal attire:

Trumpet A slim, fitted skirt or dress that flares out at the knee to create a conical trumpet shape.

A-line The skirt falls gently from the hips and flares at the hemline to create an A-shape.

Fishtail A panel sewn on to the back of the skirt simulates a fishtail.

Straight A dress that falls from the hips straight down to the hemline with no diversions.

Necklines

The neckline is the part of the dress that draws attention to and flatters your neck, shoulders, and décolletage. It is important to select a neckline that enhances your upper body while drawing the eyes of your onlookers to where they should be focused—your face.

Jewel This is similar to the look of a T-shirt; it's round and sits on the base of your throat.

Bateau This neckline follows the contour of the collarbone from the tip of one shoulder to the other with a slight dip in front.

Sweetheart This sculpted neckline is shaped like the top of a heart.

Portrait This popular look is usually in an off-the-shoulder style. It falls in a soft scoop that frames the shoulders.

V-neck This plunges to a "V" shape in the front of your dress.

Scooped Neck This lays flat and forms a soft scoop in front and back, spanning from shoulder to shoulder.

Band	This is an upright collar like a mock turtle-neck, which circles the base of the neck
Strapless	This totally reveals the neck and shoulders by eliminating the straps and sleeves.
Square	This forms a half square along the neckline
Halter	The neckline scoops in front and fastens behind the back of the neck, leaving the arms and back bare.
Tank	This has a U-shaped neckline, thin straps and deep armholes.

Sleeves

Choose your sleeves for comfort as well as style. A flattering sleeve can enhance your overall look by camouflaging heavy or thin arms, and balancing out your silhouette. But, keep in mind that the combination of improperly fitted sleeves with a tight fitted bodice can mean that movement in your gown could become restricted. Some sleeves may even restrict movement when dancing or reaching, which should be an important consideration to brides who are a bit shorter then their grooms.

Cap  These sleeves are short and fitted. They're usually paired with a fitted bodice. Although they traditionally cover only the shoulders, off-the-shoulder dresses will often incorporate a small sleeve cap, as well.

Three-quarter  This is a fitted sleeve that ends midway between the elbow and the wrist.

Fitted  This natural set-in sleeve can be either long or short. It is always without fullness and worn very close to the arm.

Pagoda

This sleeve is fitted from the shoulder to the elbow, then flares out in a tier to mid arm in front and to the wrist in back.

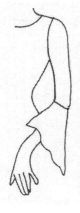

Bell   This set in sleeve is fitted from the armhole to the elbow, flaring out at the wrist.

Sleeveless   No sleeve.

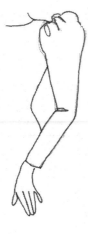

Pouf   Full and gathered at the shoulder and upper arm creating a "pouf" shape, then narrowing down towards the elbow and wrist

Waistline

The waistline brings shape and balance to your gown and adds style to your silhouette.

Natural

The bodice and skirt are joined and fitted naturally at the waist.

Basque

This has an elongated bodice, which fits through the waist and drops to a pointed "V" in front.

Dropped

The bodice is dropped to several inches below the natural waistline.

Empire

This has a shortened bodice with a high-waisted seam just below the bustline.

Chapter 10
The Train

For many women, a long train accompanies their ideal wedding gown extending from the back of their dress. However, although they might add a majestic touch, trains are not for everyone.

Many contemporary Afrocentric and heirloom styles have trains, but, usually traditional and alternative styles will not. Trains can be a few feet long up to many yards long; and extend from the waist or the shoulders all the way down to the floor. Although they are very elegant, they can also be cumbersome and difficult to get used to. Trains that are detachable offer more flexibility throughout the reception.

If your train is extremely long, such as a cathedral, you might consider having a child attendant as a "train bearer" to make sure it is beautifully displayed as you walk down the aisle.

Train Lengths:

Sweep	Extends back 8 to 12 inches after touching the floor.
Chapel	Extends 3 ½ to 4 ½ feet from the waist.
Semi-Cathedral	Extends 4 ½ to 5 ½ feet from the waist.
Cathedral	Extends 6 ½ to 7 ½ feet from the waist.

Other options that you may have are:

Watteau	Extends from the back shoulder down to floor.
Panel	This is a separate panel of fabric extending from the waist that acts as a train.

A Perfect Bride is More Than a Pretty Face...

Chapter 11

What Color Will Your Dress Be?

Although the majority of brides today still get married in some shade of ivory or white, there are no standard rules when you wear an Afrocentric wedding dress. Almost any color is acceptable and just a matter of choice. Since African-Americans come in a variety of different shades from the light almond to deep chocolate, it is important to keep your skin tone in mind when shopping for your wedding dress. You'll want to choose a color that gives your complexion a nice glow—not a sallow or dull tinge. The best way to decide what color is most flattering on you is to hold the various fabrics up against your skin.

Shades of white can vary from bright white, white with tints of blue and antique white. The actual shade will vary depending on the actual fabric. For example, stark white is bright and crisp and is best achieved with synthetic fabrics like satin and taffeta. Natural white is the whitest white you can get with natural fibers like silk. Ivory, also referred to as cream, can have slight yellow undertones giving it a creamy look. Natural silk fabrics like champagne and rum have pink undertones.

XXXXXXXXXXXX

As a bride, you can actually choose any color for your Afrocentric wedding that suits your fancy. If a combination looks good to you, and seems to go together; don't hesitate to use it because it hasn't been done before. *You may want to ask for a few other opinions, though.*

You may be a modern bride who opts to wear colors, staying far away from the American traditions. For your informal, non-traditional weddings, you could choose vibrant shades of red, purple, and orange, as well as variations of silver and gold.

If you would like a diversion from white or ivory colors and still keep your look soft and tranquil, you may want to consider wearing pastels. Peach, mauve, lavender, yellow, and baby blue look really beautiful against most skin tones of African-American women. These pale shades have grown in popularity among many brides for the entire wedding dress or as an accent color.

Most brides and grooms who prefer to wear authentic African attire seldom choose white (and gold) for their wedding ensemble. One of the most beautiful things about wearing traditional African wedding attire is the variation in color selections and the different designs that can be incorporated into your overall look.

Chapter 12
Wedding Fabrics

While most traditional Afrocentric wedding dresses are made from authentic African fabrics, satins and silks are, by far, the most popular wedding choices for the contemporary Afrocentric bride. They can be worn in every climate, every season and every time of day; and are easy to mix with ethnic trims and adornments.

Afrocentric wedding dresses can be made from a variety of fabrics, a lot of which come in 100% natural fibers as well as synthetic man-made blends. However, usually the synthetic fabrics feel much stiffer and are much less expensive. Some textiles are elegantly hand-woven and imported from Africa; other more traditional textiles are manufactured and sold generally in the United States. Oftentimes, they are combined, varying in weights and textures. There are many blends, finishes and fiber contents found in bridal fabrics that can be worn all year long, with the exceptions of velvets, mainly worn in the winter, and linens, worn in the summer.

Keep in mind that not all fabrics will work with every silhouette; and the fabric you choose should depend on the style of your wedding dress.

Recommended Fabrics for Afrocentric Wedding Gowns

Charmeuse   A lustrous, smooth, slinky fabric in silk or polyester that drapes beautifully, charmeuse is a common weave with silk or rayon and has less body then traditional silk fabrics. It is also known as a lightweight version of satin, but with a softer and clingier look.

Chiffon   This is a delicate, flowing, sheer lightweight weave made of either silk or rayon fabric.

Organza   This is a sheer, stiff or crisp fabric that's similar to chiffon but is made of a more closely woven fabric with more body.

Shantung   This is a heavier silk fabric with a rough texture and an irregular, nubby surface. Shantung can be made in 100% silk or polyester weaves. There is also a satin shantung fabric, which is a man-made blend with a silk-like finish. While similar to dupioni, shantung has a softer and lighter weight.

Tulle   This is a fine netting made of silk, nylon or rayon. Used primarily for veils and crinolines (underskirts), tulle can be found in various weaves, which either increase or decrease the weight of the fabric.

Satin   Typically made from man-made fabrics like polyester, satin is probably the most common bridal gown fabric weave. This fabric is tightly woven to create a sheen on one side. It can be found in silk-face, which is the most expensive or in blends, which are less costly. They can be shiny or in a matte finish with a toned down glow. Satin used to be made exclusively in silk; but, now the fabric can be found in polyester blends such as poly-silk satin and silky satin.

There is also a Duchess satin (also referred to as silk faced satin) that is a blend of silk and polyester (or rayon) woven into a satin finish.

Silk	This can be 100% pure or blended into chiffon, charmeuse, faille, organza, taffeta, crepe de chine, broadcloth, brocade, or peau de soie—all which have a lustrous finish and rich feel. This is the premier wedding fabric for softness, luster and beauty.
Rayon	This fabric is made from plant fibers, which come in an array of different patterns and finishes.
Crepe	A thin, lightweight fabric with a rigid or finely crinkled surface, it is made of either polyester or silk.
Dupioni	This is a silk blend with course fibers woven into a crisply textured fabric with many visible natural stubs.
Faille	This is a ribbed fabric with structure and body. Most faille comes from silk, cotton, rayon or polyester.
Gazar	This is a variation of organza, which provides a sheer effect with a stiff or starched feel.
Georgette	This is a form of crepe with a dull texture.
Jersey	This is a machine knitted blend, which can be made from a variety of fabrics, including silk, rayon and nylon, making it fluid and easy to drape.
Velvet	This is a woven fabric with a thick nap, available in cotton or rayon blends. Crushed velvet, is a variation of this blend, made with a high or low nap to give a shimmering effect.
Linen	This is a cloth made from flax fiber, which varies in coarseness from that of a fine cambric to that of a rough canvass.

Recommended Fabrics For Traditional African Weddings

There are many factors in how you choose your Afrocentric style. The fabric you choose is probably the most significant. Bear in mind that the way a gown moves and molds to your body is determined by the fabric from which it is constructed. So, whatever fabric you select, you should understand that it will give your gown its character and become the catalyst for your overall style selection.

Even though you are having a Traditional African wedding, you are not compelled to use African fabric. You should mainly choose fabric according to the design of the outfit. In some cases, you may even opt to match the color and print of your gown with your groom's suit.

If you and your fiancé are planning to wear traditional African attire or a contemporary style made from African fabric, both the bride and groom's fabric, color and print should match even if the styles of the garments are different.

Types of African Fabric

Satin Organza   From West Africa, this solid color fabric has gold embroidery.

Kente Cloth   This fabric is the symbol of the Ashanti kingdom in Ghana. These colorful embroidered strips of fabric are sewn together to create yardage.

George   This is made in India and worn by the Ibo people in Nigeria. The solid-colored fabric has gold threads woven throughout.

Aso-oke Cloth   This is probably one of the most expensive African fabrics. It is a heavy handwoven fabric from Nigeria and is usually made of cotton or silk, which comes in two forms. It has eyelet holes and is embroidered with different colored shiny threads. The more contemporary aso-oke has a shiny, metallic finish, while the older, more authentic blend is matte.

Brocade   This is a heavy cotton fabric intricately interwoven with designs such as flowers, and Adinkra symbols. It comes in a variety of colors and is found in West African countries like Senegal, Guinea and The Ivory Coast.

Rabal cloth   This woven fabric is available in 8" wide strips. It is usually used as trimming or sewn together to create fabric that can be cut and designed. You can find rabal cloth in black and silver or black and gold.

Bogolan   A hand-painted mud cloth from Mali. Bogolan or mud cloth comes in several earth tones such as deep brown, sienna, and russet. It is mostly used as trimming or for the groom's vest, tie, and/or cummerbund.

The bridesmaids and groomsmen can either wear the same (print) fabric or they can all wear different color prints. This will make the ceremony nicely personal and allow each member of the wedding party to be comfortable with his or her own individual style.

Chapter 13
Decorative Trims

As an Afrocentric bride, you can capture the feel of our culture by using a variety of trims, which include:

Lace

Lace is a patterned fabric of fine netting made with cotton, silk or nylon threads woven in ornamental designs. It is either hand-finished or machine made with or without scalloped edges. Lace comes in hundreds of weaves and colors. It can be heavy or lightweight with raised or flat motifs in floral sprays, foliage or geometric patterns. For Afrocentric wedding dresses, it is usually used as a trim, adding subtle details to your gown; however, it can also be used from head to toe and adorned with ethnic ornaments.

Shells

Cowrie shells, which symbolize female fertility, wealth and prosperity are the most widely used decorative trim for Afrocentric wedding dresses. The most recognized African ornament in the United States, cowrie shells come in different sizes and are valued for their durability and shape. They can be used natural or hand painted to create ornate designs throughout your wedding dress.

> Decorative trims are the cornerstones in defining your Afrocentric wedding dress.

Hand-painted Appliqués or Embroidery

Khemetic symbols (created from Egyptian hieroglyphics) and Adinkra symbols (representing religious beliefs of the Akan peoples of Ghana and Cote' d'Ivoire) are great ways to incorporate spiritual meanings and messages of love, peace, devotion and God to your wedding attire and throughout the wedding theme. Embroidered or hand-painted Adinkra symbols or Khemetic symbols can add a distinct African spirit to your dress, making it something more then a bridal gown. Thus, these gowns send communications—from spiritual messages to the message of love—between the bride and groom.

Beadwork

Beads were treasured in Africa more then in any other part of the world. They have been used as adornments for thousands of years.

Beads are worn as an essential part of everyday and ceremonial dress, to signify ethnic affiliation, age, marital status and wealth; and to express cultural heritage. They became essential elements of personal adornment in almost every African society where artistic expression focuses on ornamenting the body. Beads are available in a variety of colors that blend beautifully with pearls and crystals, and which can be used to coordinate with your wedding colors.

The forms and colors of beads change constantly and vary from region to region.

Types of beads include: glass, clay, coral, plastic, gold and ivory. They come in a variety of colors and numerous shapes, such as: cylinders, cubes, spheres, cones, ellipsoids and prisms.

North Africa

❀ Enormous amounts of colorful beads are worn in North Africa.

❀ Turag Crosses, which are decorative metal crosses usually cast in silver, are worn to symbolize luck, protection and power; as well as necklaces made of large, variously shaped beads from amber, coral, amazonite, silver and glass.

❀ In Egypt, colorful glass beads are used to embellish the beauty of their gold castings.

Eastern Africa

❀ In East Africa, Kenyan craftsmen make faceted aluminum, copper beads and iron beads from cast bar stock, along with wood, glass and shells.

❀ For centuries, Ethiopian silversmiths who are among the finest in Africa, have hammered or cast beads into a variety of shapes.

❀ In Somalia, Amber beads are used as a valuable wedding dowry.

Southern Africa

❀ Personal adornments have long been the predominant mode of artistic expression in South Africa, and beadwork, specifically, is an important art form of the region. Tiny round beads became especially popular amongst South African Zulu and Ndebele tribes, which use small glass seeds to create distinct and elaborate beadwork.

West Africa

❀ In West Africa, highly decorative glass beads featuring flowers, stripes and mosaic designs, which appeal to the people's love of bright colors, are used in both clothing and jewelry.

❀ In West African, gold beads are made, using the "lost-wax" casting process.

❀ West Africa is also known for its gold and ivory.

❀ Benin uses amber, coral and glass beads

❀ Nigeria uses a variety of cylindrical and double-drilled stone beads.

❀ Mali uses stone beads made of granite.

❀ The Ivory Coast uses round pottery beads.

❀ Ghana uses Bodom beads, which are thought to have medicinal powers. These beads are usually yellow, and often decorated with red, blue, green and brown paint colors.

❀ Cameroon uses glass beads, which were often interspersed with those of gold.

Chapter 14
Accentuating Your Body Type

Every bride dreams of being the perfect vision of elegance, style, and beauty on her wedding day; and selecting the right gown can make that dream come true. Fortunately wedding gowns, like brides, come in different shapes and sizes. Choosing an Afro centric wedding gown that flatters your body type is just as important as your personal style. The biggest mistake you can make is selecting a gown with design elements that are not complimentary to your features or that completely overwhelm you.

To capture your own best look, you'll need to keep an open mind and be objective about your physical features. It is not important to follow trends when selecting your gown; but, it is pertinent to choose a dress that is comfortable and flattering for your body type. As a bridal wear designer, I always recommend that you take a totally honest evaluation of your body parts; because, let's face it; not everything looks good on everybody.

Choose a wedding gown that works for your shape and flatters what, you believe, are your best assets. Your wedding dress should be made specifically to enhance and beautify your form. It is fantasy wrapped in fabric.

Before you shop, ask yourself these pertinent questions. What about your body type? Are you tall or short? Big boned or small? Busty or small breasted? Is your waistline small or large? Do you want to show off your shoulders or upper arms or keep them covered. If you are conscious about a specific part of your body, like your bust, arms or hips, take this into consideration when you shop. Be realistic about your body shape; but don't be too hard on your self, because there *is* an ideal Afrocentric wedding dress for your specific shape.

Wedding Fashions for Full Figure Brides

There are many new Afrocentric wedding gown styles emerging, that have been designed to flatter full-figured brides; such as: off-the-shoulder gowns with bell sleeves, fitted bodices and slimming A-line skirts. The wide variety should make your selection optically easy and give your figure a perfect illusion. Here are some specifics for you to consider when you're shopping for your perfect Afrocentric wedding gown:

The Best Dress Shapes

❊ If you choose to wear a sheath style, make sure it is very well made and well-fitted. A sheath gown can actually make you look a lot slimmer than a fitted gown.

❊ Try a dress with a basque waist and full skirt. This style has a slimming effect and de-emphasizes your hips.

❊ Empire waists and A-line styles work well for full-figured women.

❊ Because of the wrapping and layering of fabric, traditional African attire always works well to camouflage a not so slender body shape.

The Best Necklines

❊ Select a neckline such as V, square, jewel or bateau. These will de-emphasize your bustline and flatter your figure.

❊ Scooped necklines or off-the-shoulder necklines, accenting a princess / A-line shape, will elongate your body, giving you the illusion of height and slimness.

The Best Sleeve Styles

❊ Fitted sleeves are a better choice than puff or full sleeves

❊ Bell sleeves look great on your plus-size figure, because they'll slim you're your upper arms, by drawing attention to the exaggerated sleeve opening.

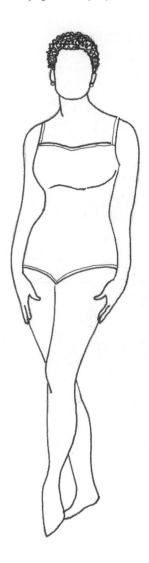

Do's for Full Figured Brides

❊ Wear a stunning headpiece with a non-exaggerated veil to bring attention to your face.

❊ Wear supportive undergarments.

Don'ts for Full Figured Brides

❊ Avoid contrasting colors and clingy fabrics.

❊ Do not wear fitted sleeves on your arms. Choose something with some fullness or a longer length sleeve.

❊ Avoid gowns with too much fabric and detail near your face.

❊ Avoid bulky fabrics like velvets and heavy satins.

❊ Avoid wearing shiny fabrics. Instead select matte satins or silks and lightweight crepes.

Wedding Fashions for Petite Brides

The illusion of height is often a key consideration for petite brides who are five feet four and under; and long, lean silhouettes will usually make you look taller. I find that, as long as your gown is made in proportion to your body, petite brides can wear just about any style.

The Best Dress Shapes

❋ Silhouettes that look best on petite brides include A-lines and sheath styles.

❋ Princess lines and the long unbroken vertical seams give you the illusion of added height.

❋ Wear a sheath or empire style dress; these shapes elongate your body with a sleek silhouette.

❋ Slim silhouettes add length; simple, sleek lines elongate your body.

The Best Necklines

❋ Necklines like sweetheart and off-the-shoulder styles are very flattering for you.

❋ Consider a dress with detailing around the neckline to call attention to your face.

The Best Sleeves

❋ Cap sleeves are good choices for you.

Do's for Petite Brides

✿ Your veil length should be short and waist-skimming or shoulder skimming.

✿ Look for small delicate details.

✿ You can also wear a taller headpiece such as a "kufi" style to add height.

Don'ts for Petite Brides

✿ For your small, trim figure, you'll want to keep your Afrocentric wedding dress simple. Don't add too much volume or ornamentation.

✿ Avoid dress styles that involve large amounts of fabric; this will only swallow up your petite figure.

✿ Avoid drop waist bodices. They make your torso look too long; and your legs look too short.

✿ Don't wear a ballgown style wedding gown; you will look overwhelmed.

Wedding Fashions for Tall & Thin Brides

Most tall brides, five feet nine inches and over, have unlimited choices. You can wear whatever Afrocentric style bridal gown you want. **The most important factors are that you feel comfortable, and that your gown is appropriate for the atmosphere you desire to create.**

The Best Dress Shapes

❋ Ballgown shapes with a fuller skirt will minimize your height, lend some curves and add fullness to your figure.

❋ The straight sheath is a classic, contemporary style, but it is not good if you are extremely flat chested.

❋ Define your waist with princess styles that curve outward at your waistline.

The Best Necklines

❋ Accent your collarbone with a fitted bodice and open neckline.

The Best Sleeves

❋ Choose a sleeve that extends your shoulder line like portrait and **bateau** collars.

Do's for Tall & Thin Brides

❋ Long veils work well.

❋ Horizontal details are perfect for you.

Don'ts for Tall & Thin Brides

❋ Avoid dresses with dropped waistlines and torsos.

❋ Do not wear a silhouette with a high neckline and long sleeves.

Wedding Fashions for Brides with Heavy Hips: (Pear-shaped)

If you have been blessed with a smaller upper body and a larger lower body, you would be considered "pear-shaped". Your bust is usually small, your shoulders are narrow, and your waist is defined. When selecting your Afrocentric wedding gown, pay close attention to styles that can add balance to your body's proportions.

The Best Dress Shapes

- ✸ An A-line or ballgown is ideal for a pear-shape. You should balance this with a fitted bodice, an off-the-shoulder neckline, or a portrait collar.

- ✸ Basque or dropped waistlines with full skirts and peplums will camouflage your hips and derriere.

- ✸ A fitted waist adds definition. Paired with an A-line skirt, it will hide extra inches.

- ✸ If you want to wear a train over a slim skirt, camouflage your hips with train attachments.

The Best Necklines

- ✸ Off-the-shoulder necklines and elaborate bodices will accentuate your upper body

- ✸ Select a dress with an illusion top that emphasizes the line of the shoulders.

The Best Sleeves

- ✸ Try full sleeve treatments or small shoulder pads to extend your upper body.

Do's: Heavy Hips

- ❀ Purchase a girdle or corset that flattens the stomach and emphasizes the waist.

- ❀ Bodice tops with peplum hemlines will draw attention away from the derriere.

- ❀ Do wear stiffer fabrics below your waistline to help you achieve a trim tailored shape.

Don'ts: Heavy Hips

- ❀ Don't wear an oversized shoulder pad to balance out your hips.

- ❀ Avoid body hugging sheaths, horizontal lines and heavy gathering at the hip area.

- ❀ Avoid empire styles dresses.

Wedding Styles for the Bride with a Long Torso and Short Legs

If your body is long and narrow; and your shoulders and hips are very close in size with not much of a waist, you should create a long, uninterrupted silhouette. Do not choose an Afrocentric wedding gown style that has a well-defined bodice, waist or skirt.

The Best Dress Shapes

❀ A straight sheath style with a cutout back would be very flattering on you. It camouflages your waist.

❀ An empire style will draw attention away from your waistline.

The Best Necklines

❀ A dress with a low neckline will work well to shorten your torso, and make it look more in proportion to your legs.

The Best Sleeves

❀ Try puff sleeves to add more accent to your pleasing silhouette.

Do's: Long Torso and Short Legs

❀ Select an ankle length or floor length dress.

Don'ts Long Torso and Short Legs

❀ Do not wear a dress with an elongated torso.

❀ Avoid dresses with defined waistlines.

Wedding Styles for the Bride with Heavy Arms

The Best Dress Shapes

❋ Sheath styles create a vertical silhouette and draw attention away from your sleeves.

The Best Necklines

❋ Select a dress with an interesting neckline, such as sweetheart or jewel ; this will draw attention away from your arms.

The Best Sleeves

❋ Choose sleeves that are elbow or wrist length with natural shoulder lines and no padding.

Do's: Heavy Arms

❁ Select styles that de-emphasis your shoulders and arms.

❁ Try something lightweight like lace above your waistline.

❁ Choose styles that feature peplums or other horizontal details at the waistline or hip.

Don'ts: Heavy Arms

❁ Stay away from horizontal detailing in the upper bodice.

❁ Avoid cap sleeves, off-the-shoulder and strapless styles or full, puffed sleeves.

❁ Avoid heavy fabrics above your waistline.

Wedding Styles for the Small Breasted Bride

If you have small breasts, you should draw attention away from your bust by wearing interesting necklines and using exquisite fabrics. You should also consider wearing a push-up bra or bra cups under your Afrocentric wedding dress for a bigger boost.

The Best Dress Shapes

❋ Balance out your silhouette with a flowing skirt that drapes your figure in a flattering way.

❋ An empire waist wedding gown will create a natural definition around your bust.

The Best Necklines

❋ Take the emphasis off your chest and highlight your collarbone with an open, off the shoulder neckline.

The Best Sleeves

❋ Your sleeves should be in proportion to your arms—nothing too overpowering, but more on the slim or delicate side.

Do's: Small Breasts

❋ Choose a dress style with a dramatic, cutout back and a cinched waist.

❋ If you choose to wear a strapless gown, then add beading or a silk or satin cuff at your bustline for more definition.

❋ Opt for a dress with a yoke cut within the bodice, around the bustline and use a different fabric in this area. Pleated fabrics or lace would look great and works wonders here.

Don'ts: Small Breasts

❋ Don't wear plain, fitted bodices, even if you create a bustline shape. This will look too artificial.

Wedding Styles for the Voluptuous and Busty Bride

Brides with really curvy figures should be delighted to show them off. Your bust and hip measurements are very close but your waist is noticeably smaller then your hips. You should look for an Afrocentric wedding gown style that can either accentuate your God-given attributes, without appearing to be too sensual.

The Best Dress Shapes

- The halter style will support your full bustline.
- A fitted bodice with a jewel neckline and cap sleeves, balanced with a full skirt will emphasize your waistline, not your bust.

The Best Necklines

- A "V" neckline is the perfect eye-catcher to top of your Afrocentric wedding gown.

The Best Sleeves

- An open neckline and off-the-shoulder sleeves flatter the shoulders and add width to the upper body.

Do's: Large Breasts

- Make sure you choose a foundation garment that is uplifting and supportive.
- Look for natural or slightly dropped waist.
- Choose a soft silk skirt to balance a lightly embellished bodice.

Don'ts: Large Breasts

- Avoid high necklines, empire waists and elongated torsos—which can throw off your proportion.

Wedding Styles for the Brides With Broad Shoulders—"T" Shaped

You have broad shoulders and a large bust, with slender hips and legs. Quite naturally, you are probably seeking to de-emphasize the top of your body and accentuate your hips and legs. I've made some very flattering Afrocentric wedding gown styles for brides with similar proportions. Here are some suggestions for you, too.

The Best Dress Shapes

❀ Select a dress, such as an A-line silhouette, with a narrow bodice that offsets your shoulders and creates a fabulous hourglass shape.

❀ Balance your figure with a full skirt and fitted bodice.

The Best Necklines

❀ An off the shoulder neckline with long sleeves will play up your beautiful broad shoulders and give you a truly elegant look.

❀ V-necklines will reduce your upper body width.

❀ Halters look great on broad shoulders and athletic builds.

The Best Sleeves

❀ Look for simple sleeves that will flatter your natural shoulder-line.

✿✿✿✿✿✿✿✿✿✿✿

Do's: Broad Shoulders

❀ Broad shoulders are great! You should expose them.

Don'ts: Broad Shoulders

❀ Avoid narrow skirts and severe necklines that draw the eye upward.

Chapter 15
Investing In Your Wedding Gown

Depending on whether you have your gown made, buy it off the rack, or make it yourself the investment can vary tremendously. You must work around the budget you have allocated for your dress. This will help you decide the best route to take.

It can be difficult to go into a bridal salon and find an Afrocentric wedding dress; the mainstream bridal companies and stores do not cater to this niche. This means you have one of three options:

1. There are designers, like myself, who specialize in Afrocentric bridal attire with a vast selection to choose from.

2. Find a store specializing in Ethnic clothing and ask them to assist you in making your gown.

3. Or buy a dress, off-the-rack, and embellish it yourself, giving it an Afrocentric flare.

In any event, if you are opting for an Afrocentric style, you should have some idea by now of the design elements needed for your desired look. I have elaborated on the fundamentals of having your gown custom made versus buying your gown "off the rack".

> ✤✤✤✤✤✤✤✤✤
> Buying a wedding gown is an investment that won't be recouped, but it can give you more joy than most decisions you'll ever make in your lifetime.

Having Your Wedding Gown Custom-Made

Having your wedding dress made by a designer provides more flexibility and versatility in your style choices. If you have a theme in mind, but are not quite sure how to execute it, working with a designer will be quite a unique experience and can help bring your ideas together.

For the discerning bride–to-be, having a gown custom-made is an ideal way of ensuring you get the wedding gown of your dreams that also fits you perfectly. One of the advantages of choosing a custom-made gown is that you can create a dress that is unique to you, with all the design elements you like, made to fit your body, in the colors and fabrics you want.

Sometimes the cost of a custom-made gown is a stumbling block for brides. Due to the many circumstances, the average price for custom made gowns starts at about $2,000.00 and up. Custom-made gowns are quite different from those purchased from off-the-rack. They are made one at a time, especially for your body measurements and specifications; and are not constructed from standard sized patterns. All tailoring and alterations are made exclusively in the process of preparing your custom-made gown, with numerous man-hours and great attention to the finishing. So, when you put all this into perspective, it seems well worth it.

It takes considerable skill and patience to achieve that all-important look and fit, so make sure you find a dressmaker or designer who you are comfortable working with.

Choosing between a designer and a dressmaker depends on your budget and your needs. Designers start from scratch, consulting with you and creating a dress for you depending on your specifications. They will sketch it out for you and provide you with swatches of fabric and trims to be used to make your dress. A designer will either sew the dress personally or hire a seamstress to sew the dress. A dressmaker will make your gown to order, according to your specifications. You would provide the design or pattern, as well as the fabric and trim; and it would be custom fitted to you.

Your designer should design your wedding dress exclusively for you, based on your personal needs. So, if you are having your gown custom-made, you should sit down with your designer and answer the following questions:

* What do you want to feel like on your wedding day? (Regal? Sexy?)

* Where is the wedding taking place (Church? Home, Caribbean Island?)

* What you are going to be doing on your wedding day? (Dancing? Jumping the Broom? Kneeling?)

Before your initial appointment with a designer or dress-maker, key in on the fundamentals of the dress or gown that you would like, and plan to discuss them with the designer. You should have some idea about what silhouette, neckline, sleeve and bodice you would feel most comfortable wearing. For example, what neckline, bodice and sleeve style would enhance your figure? Make sure you have an idea of the silhouette you want to wear and the desired length of the gown. How formal will your wedding be and do you want to wear a train? You can get great ideas by looking through bridal magazines for flattering silhouettes.

Then, decide what elements of African culture you would like to incorporate. You should collect photos, fabric swatches and any other references that you can find to aid your designer or dressmaker in creating your unique wedding dress. Culturally oriented books will help you with suggestions on how to pull your look together.

Depending on the elements incorporated into your dress, the price range for having a gown designed and made specifically for you will vary from each designer. Make sure that if you choose this option, there are no additional, "hidden" charges (i.e. for being plus size or tall etc.) The price that designers quote you should be what it is. Be sure you confirm, in writing, exactly what you are getting before you start.

Fittings

Fittings are a necessary part of your wedding preparation. Your wedding dress should be fitted perfectly to your body. Plan to have at least three fittings, beginning anywhere from nine months to six months before the wedding.

1st fitting	Muslin fitting (for contour and shape)
2nd fitting	Actual fabric fitting (for fabric reaction and tailoring)
3rd fitting	Final fitting (for comfort and final changes)

The average time to make a wedding dress is 6 to 9 months. However, your wedding gown should never be completed until 4 to 6 weeks before your wedding date, just in case you lose or gain a little bit of weight.

Custom-made gowns require a least three fittings. The first fitting is a mock-up version of your dress. It is made using detailed measurements based on your body specifications. At this stage, minor details such as depth of neckline, length of sleeves or train etc. can be altered along with tailoring the dress shape to compliment your figure.

The second fitting is usually done in the actual fabric that your dress is being made from, in which minor alterations are made.

And the third fitting is for final approval of the overall fit and comfort.

The Therez Fleetwood Bridal Collection, which incorporates many different regions of Africa, has been influenced by the variety of artwork and adornments found throughout the vast Continent.

You, too, can take influences from the different regions of Africa and apply your favorite adornments to your perfect wedding gown.

Losing Weight

Are you planning to lose weight before your wedding? If so, you must inform the designer or seamstress making or tailoring your dress. Then, try to lose that weight before your first fitting and do your best to maintain your desired weight.

When you have about 10-15 pounds to lose, this is easy to do on your own. There are several diets that work—you must find the one that's right for you based on your dietary needs. And remember to make exercise a part of your weight loss plan. Dieting will help you lose the weight and exercise will help you keep your body toned.

If you want to lose more than ten pounds, seek out a professional weight control service, such as Jenny Craig, Weight Watchers or Well 4 Life. They will set up a personal program that gets you where you want to be in a reasonable amount of time. The money is well worth it.

Never, never, starve yourself. It can destroy your health. And, don't feel pressure to become someone you are not! After all, your fiancé proposed to you the way you are.

The Budgeting Bride

If you are on a budget and cannot afford the expense of a custom-made Afrocentric wedding dress, then you may want to buy a less expensive dress that you can adorn yourself. When purchasing a dress off-the-rack, look for a clean, simple silhouette, where Afrocentric adornments can be easily applied.

Come up with a budget before you start shopping. You should have an approximate price for the total cost of your wedding dress in mind. Then decide on the trims you would like to use, such as: cowrie shells, beads, African fabrics, and embroidery, silver or gold trinkets. Next, calculate the amount of trims you need and the cost of these items. Also, consider that if you or a family member cannot handsew these trims onto your dress, you will have to add the cost of hiring a seamstress into the total cost of your dress.

When shopping for an off-the-rack bridal gown, you'll discover that there is tremendous variation in the quality of the fabrics and the construction. It is best to buy a gown made from sturdy fabrics such as satin, taffeta or a heavy weight silk. They will hold their shape and structure when applying adornments to your gown. However, mass-produced dresses used in the bridal market today are usually made out of *man-made fibers,* which consist of nylon, acetate and polyester, which are the less expensive fabrics.

When trying on ready made wedding gowns, be cautious of the fit of the dress. A lot of African-American women's bodies are basically two sizes. If you are larger on top, than on the bottom, buy the dress to fit your bodice and have the hip and waistline tailored to your shape, or vice-versa. It is a lot easier to take in a larger dress than it is to let out a dress that is too small. In most instances, if you buy a wedding dress "off the rack," there will probably be alterations that need to be made to enhance your figure. If so, you should make the alterations to your dress first, then apply the ethnic trims.

Most traditional African wedding attire is pretty affordable because these silhouettes are basically three pieces of fabric (2 to 3 yards each) that wrap around the body. These fabric pieces consist of a wrap skirt, a shawl and gele. The only constructed item in traditional wedding attire is the shirt.

On the other hand, contemporary and alternative styles are more constructed garments, which are usually more expensive. They required several pattern pieces, a more intricate sewing process, lining, tailoring, darting and boning. But, you can add a variety of African motifs to a simple elegant silhouette. Working with a plain, solid color dress is like creating artwork on a clean canvas. The sky's the limit!

Another way to add Afrocentric elegance to your overall look is to purchase a simple, but elegant gown and dress it up with culturally inspired jewelry or a fabulous dramatic headpiece. For an heirloom gown, you can add your grandmother's brooch as a centerpiece; and then add beads, crystals or gems to enhance the beauty of this special piece of jewelry.

Chapter 16
The Crowning Achievement

Veils

Although some African-American brides choose to wear very little on their heads or in their hair on their wedding day, nothing signifies her more then her veil. However, wearing a veil on your wedding day is optional and strictly a matter of personal choice.

There are many types of veils to select from and your decision should be made according to your height and the style of the gown you have selected, as well as the surroundings for your wedding. Veils come in all styles and lengths that range from the tip of your nose to the tip of your train. They are usually made of fabrics such as tulle, lace, chiffon, illusion or organza. Some are fashioned simply with a single layer of netting, or elaborately with multiple layers of netting. The veiling is usually attached to the headpiece using snaps, velcro or combs.

Maintain Your Uniqueness
Your headpiece and veil are accessories that are unique to your Afrocentric wedding style. You'll want them to complement your face shape and coordinate with your gown.

Veils can be plain or unfinished, and trimmed with a narrow piece of ribbon or satin cording. You can embellish your veil by using a variety of trims, such as: lace, cowrie shells or flowers; hand painted Adinkra symbols or hieroglyphics; ribbons, beads, stones or embroidery. If you choose a tulle veil, there are variations to consider. The softer fabric has a nicer draping effect. However, if you prefer a stiffer tulle, I suggest that you 'scallop' the edges to give it a softer appearance than the typical straight corners.

Basic Veil Terms

Blusher or Illusion, 27"	Can be worn over the face as the bride walks down the aisle. It is a short, chin-length veil worn over the face that is turned back over the headpiece after the ceremony. It can be attached to a longer veil or hat.
Waist, 30"	Falls to the waist.
Shoulder length	Touches the shoulders and is usually worn with an informal gown.
Flyaway	An informal veil that consists of several layers of stiff tulle that grazes the shoulders and is usually worn with an informal gown.
Elbow, 34"	Falls to the elbow. Worn with a short and/or informal gown.

Fingertip, 45"

Extends to the fingertips. Worn with a semi-formal gown.

Ballerina or Waltz

Falls between the knees and ankles. Worn with a formal or semi-formal gown.

Sweep, 72"

Barely sweeps the floor. This style is the same length as the dress. Worn with a semi-formal or formal gown.

Chapel Length, 102"

Falls onto the floor as a chapel train. Extends roughly 2½ yards from the headpiece, trailing slightly on the floor. Worn with a semi-formal or formal gown.

Cathedral Length, 120"

Falls to the floor as a cathedral train. Extends roughly 3½ yards from the headpiece. Worn with a formal gown.

Mantilla

Traditionally made of lace and worn with a simple, elegant, classic gown. Attached to the hair with combs and pins. Draped over the top of the bride's head.

Your Headpiece

Your headpiece is the ultimate accessory that can add culture and heritage to your Afrocentric wedding attire. If you're on a limited budget, you may choose a simple dress from a bridal salon and want to add an ornate Afrocentric headpiece to emphasize your theme.

The headpiece you choose should feel secure, be flattering and easy to wear. If you choose to work with a designer to have your headpiece custom-made, it is important that he or she considers the shape of your face and the way you are going to wear your hair. Everything should work together to create one beautiful image.

The designer will need to see either a picture or a sketch of you wedding gown in order to incorporate some type of styling that will be complementary to your overall look. The designer will also need swatches so that he or she can match the shade of white, off-white, pink, or whatever color you have chosen. This is really important because there are different shades of tulle, and fabrics take on different light depending on what the textures are. It is equally important to know what type of embellishments are used on the dress, such as: iridescent sequins, plain sequins, silver bugle beads, what kind of pearls or what kind of rhinestones. All of these elements are necessary so that they can be incorporated into the headpiece without clashing with your gown.

Sherrie Hobson-Green, a unique headpiece designer located in Brooklyn, New York, prides herself on making flexible

The Therez Fleetwood Bridal Collection

Before You Say "I Do"...

My Day—
My Way—
It's finally here. . .
The day I say
"I Do"

Love, Joy, and
Happiness...

The Therez Fleetwood Bridal Collection

You've
Made
It!

Your
Perfect
Wedding
Day

Congratulations

It's
Your
Day
and
Your
Night....

...And Your
N·U·P·T·I·A·L·S

**Bridal Designer
Therez Fleetwood**

headpieces that are expressive and fun. She has a knack of mixing Afrocentric touches with a Euro-centric feeling, knowing just what to add and what to take away to make it fabulous. Sherrie is most proud of the joy and excitement that radiates from her clients when they see the final piece.

According to Sherrie, "I like my brides to feel, to know that they are the queen of the day, special. Every eye will be focused on them the entire day. There is not going to be one time that you see the bride and someone is not looking at her. I want her to feel her best and look her greatest, and know that she is absolutely gorgeous. I bring this out in the headpieces. The headpiece is the "dot on the I". It enhances and accents her best facial features, which are most often her eyes or her smile."

Coordinate Your Look

A simple headpiece works best with a spectacular dress and a more detailed headpiece works best with a simple dress.

Headpieces and attachments come in a variety of styles. There are decorative combs, bobby pins, headbands, hairpins, and barrettes. Even if you initially resolve to wear nothing in your hair, you may enjoy a subtle change. Try on a tiara, a fitted cap, an Afrocentric crown, or to draw attention to your eyes, simply drape some beads around your forehead. Ethnic elements, such as: cowrie shells, beads, metal trinkets, silver or gold coins, feathers, jeweled stones or even lace can add just the right touch.

With several silhouettes to select from, your choices are unlimited. You can select a tiara with delicate wiring, which incorporates cowrie shells and other beads; hairpins adorned with crystals; and silver or gold trinkets. Some of the more elaborate crowns come in a variety of shapes. One of my favorites is a Nefertiti style, which is straight with an open top and exaggerated points that delicately caress your face.

Some brides opt to wear a regal Afrocentric crown to pull their look together rather than an Afrocentric garment. Wearing this type of headpiece throughout the evening, can make a very elegant statement. The Afrocentric crown can be made in a variety of different ways and sizes. It can be worn to the front of your forehead or sit securely on the crown of your head.

The headpiece worn with traditional African attire is called a "gele" or fabric wrap—(Gele is referred to a fabric that is used to wrap headpieces, to construct a headpiece). The term loosely used could mean any headpiece.

There are so many different looks for African head wraps, that you really cannot categorize them into a particular style or type. This is what makes them so beautiful— the fact that you can wrap them in so many different ways, all of which begin with a piece of fabric that measures 2½ yards long. You can use the same fabric as the body of the dress, or you can use special headpiece fabrics. There are several different fabrics that can be used for these headpieces. In Nigeria, for example, the fabric of choice is called "haze"—a paper like fabric, which wraps well and holds its shape. It usually comes in two-tones, a basic color enhanced with gold or silver. With the "haze" you can construct several headwrap designs and be as stylish as you want to be.

In selecting your headpiece you must also consider your proportions. For example, if you are short and a little round, then you should consider a headpiece that gives you height, causing the eye to travel up to make you appear more slender. Or if you are tall, you don't want to create a piece that will add to your height and overpower your fiancé; you both should be as close to the same eye-level as possible.

It is important to try on as many headpiece styles that interest you to find the one that complements your gown, flatters your face shape and gives you a regal air. Although your headpiece should complement your gown, sometimes, selecting it can be just as confusing as choosing your gown. Just make sure the style, design and character of your headpiece gives you the "crowning effect" for your Afrocentric bridal outfit. Don't rush your decision. Once your bridal gown has been selected, you can take the necessary time to find your favorite headpiece.

Types of Headpieces:

Wreath	A band that encircles the bride's head, usually made with flowers.
Juliet Cap	A small, contoured headpiece fitted closely to the bride's head. It can be positioned either on the forehead or the back of the head.
Kufi	A head-piece, usually made from African printed fabric. (4" to 6" high)
Crown	A circlet that sits on top of your head (circular band).
Tiara	A very formal style that sits on top of the head, such as a crown-like headdress made of jewels and flowers.
Headband	A fabric-covered or beaded strip that is shaped like an arc and fits close to the head with a puffy tulle veil attached.
Gele or Headwrap	A traditional, African headwrap.
Forehead Adornments	A beaded circlet that fits the circumference of a bride's head.

Try It Before You Buy It

When you try on your headpiece, wear your hair the way you will be wearing it on your wedding day.

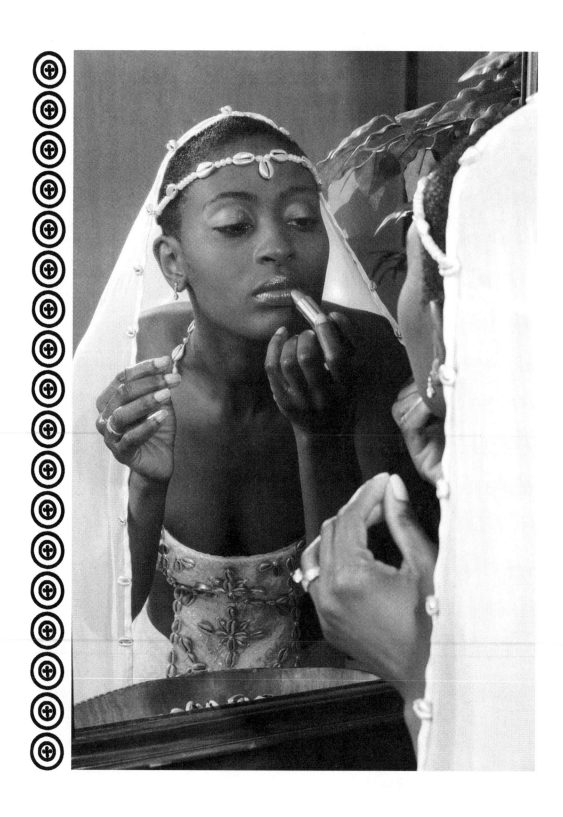

Chapter 17
A Touch of Beauty: Hair, Nails and Make-Up

Your Hairstyle

When it comes to your wedding day hairstyle, keep it simple and elegant. A good hairstylist will help you find the best look for you and will be truthful about it. He or she will take into consideration your hair type, face shape and bone structure.

If you're not sure where to go, ask your friends for their suggestions, and go to several hairstylists for a consultation. Talk about what you'll be wearing ask each hairstylist for a few different suggestions. You should try several hairstyles and look at yourself from all angles to determine what works best for you. You have to feel like yourself and be comfortable with the hairstylist. Your final hairstyle should reflect your personality.

⊕⊕⊕⊕⊕⊕⊕⊕⊕⊕⊕

Don't opt for something that will overpower you or your overall image; and never choose a hairstyle just because you've seen it in a magazine.

Have Fun With Hair Pieces

If your hair is short, you can have fun with hairpieces. Be sure to match the color of your hairpiece with your natural color.

Natural hairstyles are always a great way to incorporate your heritage into your Overall look and give you a regal air. Whether your hair is weaved, locked, braided, relaxed or cropped there are many ornate hairdos that would be appropriate.

Perhaps you might opt for a beautiful cornrowed style with beads, cowrie shells, and trims entwined or create an upswept hairstyle with goddess braids, Senegalese twists or relaxed hair. You could pull your hair up into a French twist, adorned with a collection of ornaments made from twisted wire, cowrie shells, beads, pearls, crystal and stones, with a veil attached at the back. You may choose to add flowers to your hair, with the stems clipped and inserted into your finished hairstyle or the buds wired onto a comb that's tucked creatively into your hair.

Symbolic Adornments

In Northern Africa, ornate silver jewelry is applied to the bride's braided hair. They also use shells, amber beads and gold pendants to adorn their hair. Blue beads, mean purity, white beads symbolize health, and violet beads symbolize love.

Hair Care Options

Conditioning

Conditioning and maintenance will help to assure that your wedding day hairstyle looks great on you. However, deep conditioning should not be done the day before or the day of your wedding—it may make your hair too heavy to hold a curl.

Cutting

Short, cropped styles should definitely be trimmed and have the edges cleaned up one week before your wedding day. Every two to three months, even if you are trying to grow out your hair, you should still get regular trims in order to prevent split ends. For those of you who have dry, brittle or damaged hair, you might consider getting it cut into a new style, but be sure to allow yourself enough time before your wedding day, so that you'll be comfortable with it.

Weaving

Soft, loose ringlets are "romantic and feminine…" just how most women want to feel on their wedding day. If your hair is not long enough, you might wish to get a full-head hairweave or just a partial for certain effects. In any case, hairweaving takes time and it takes some getting used to. If you've never tried it, do it at least a few weeks before your wedding day…just in case.

Coloring

Any experimentations with hair color should be tried at least six months prior to your wedding. If the effect is great you can repeat it. If it is a disaster, you have time to repair the damage; and, by all means, keep it in great condition with good products and minimal blow drying.

Relaxing

For best results, relaxers should never be done the day of or the day before your wedding—they can make your hair feel too limp. If you plan to have you hair relaxed and colored, this should be done at least 4 weeks before your wedding.

⊕⊕⊕⊕⊕⊕⊕⊕⊕⊕⊕⊕ ⊕⊕⊕⊕⊕⊕⊕⊕

Keep The Look Cohesive

As a bride you should be open to advise your bridesmaids on how to style their hair, and not always leave it up to them. Hair ornaments are always a good choice for your bridesmaids because it helps to keep a cohesive look amongst you bridal party.

Trust your judgment, plan early and you'll have a great wedding *hair-day*.

Hair Care Countdown

6 months before

Begin to take care of your hair. Be cautious of the relaxers and curling irons. If used improperly, they can cause breakage to your hair.

4 months before

Consult several hairdressers. Let them know what you have in mind. Bring in pictures of styles that you like and ask their opinion. Select the stylist you feel most comfortable with.

2 to 3 months before

Bring your headpiece to your hairdresser to make sure that the hairstyle that you have chosen works with and complements your look.

4 weeks before

This is the time for your color and cut, if you've decided to go with a new look.

2 weeks before

Get your highlights and a trim.

1 week before

See your hairstylist for a last minute trim, if necessary.

1 day before or day of

last chance to get it right for your perfect wedding day look.

Your Nails

It is best to get a manicure the day before or the morning of your wedding to assure that the polish stays neat and fresh. Whether you have long beautiful natural nails, lovely acrylic nails or very short nails, a French manicure or nude, natural nail polish works best with your wedding attire and adds a nice finishing touch.

Your Makeup

Your wedding day is not the time to experiment with makeup. Seek consultation with a professional makeup artist 4 to 6 weeks before the wedding. Tell the makeup artist the time and location of the wedding and how it will be recorded (with a photographer or videographer). A professional makeup application will cost between $20 and $50 and can make a significant difference in the way you look and how your wedding photographs will turn out.

Don't deviate much from what you wear on a day-to-day basis; but even if you don't wear makeup regularly, do it for your wedding. It will even out your skin tone, brighten your face and enhance you appearance. When choosing makeup for your wedding, the most important thing is to look like yourself and feel comfortable with that look. While someone who wears a lot should not apply makeup too heavily, you don't want it to be overpowering. You should choose colors that you would normally wear when going out. For instance, if you wear red lipstick and love it, then you can stick with that family of color for your wedding.

Since a large number of African-American brides wear white wedding gowns, it is critical that your makeup has a little more definition to avoid looking washed out. Added definition is also needed for better quality photographs. This is where a professional touch can do you great justice.

Generally makeup follows the bride's hair color. If you are blonde, soft pinks, warm peach and salmon colors work well. For brunettes, light-to-medium colors like rose, brown, berry and mahogany are nice. Redheads look great in rich browns or brown-red shades. Deep colors like dazzling reds and burgundies are perfect for the bride with black hair. Gray hair tends to drain the face, so go back to those soft shades of peach and pink.

Foundation

Use matte, oil-free, water-based foundation to even out your skin tone and reduce shine. Then set it with powder.

Eye Makeup

Eyeliner will give a nice definition to your eyes. For best results, line your eyes with eyeshadow or a powder liner. *Powder based products won't run or smudge.* Make sure the eye colors are matte (not shiny). *Frosted or iridescent eyeshadows will photograph poorly.* For lasting eye shadow and crease-proof eyelids, apply an even coating of eye makeup primer underneath the eye shadow. Use a waterproof mascara to add fullness and length to your eyelashes.

If you are not used to wearing false eyelashes, don't let anyone talk you into wearing them for the ceremony. They take some getting used to; they drastically change your persona; and having one come loose or fall off would be extremely embarrassing.

Pack A Beauty Bag

Be sure to have a beauty bag with you the day of your wedding and have your maid of honor or one of your bridesmaids hold it for you. You bag should hold all your makeup and hair essentials for touch-ups or emergencies. It should include, lipstick, translucent powder, bobby pins, a handkerchief, a small brush or comb, mints and anything else you can think of.

Lips

Your lips should be well defined. Use a lip liner to outline and then to fill in the lips with color. *This will act as a base for your lipstick.* Then, using a lip brush, apply your lipstick on top of the liner and blot. *Be careful not to go outside of the line.* Reapply your lipstick and blot it again. This will ensure that you lipstick lasts throughout the day.

Keep Your Lipstick From Smudging

For best results, use a white tissue to blot your lipstick. First, open it and press it on your lips; then fold it and place it between your lips. This will keep your lip line intact and prevent lipstick from smudging or getting on your teeth.

Blush

Your blush should be in the same family of colors as your lipstick—pink, coral, red, plum, etc. Apply a light coating directly on your cheek bones—not above, not below, and not too close to your nose. Avoid using too much blush, just enough to give you a healthy glow.

When applying makeup, be sure your gown is covered with a smock or a cloth. To avoid stains, apply the makeup first, cover the face and hair with a silk scarf, and then slip the gown over your head. If you want to go jazzier with your makeup, wait until the reception. You want to keep your look softer and more natural for the ceremony.

The Art of Mehndi (Henna Painting)

In many African societies, the bride enters a customary period of preparation for marriage. She receives beauty treatments; her hair is ceremonially washed; her body is massaged with coconut oil and perfumed with sandalwood; and her hands and feet are decorated with henna. Known for its power to protect, to bring luck, and to provide material and spiritual wealth, henna is used in ceremonies having to do with the rites of passage.

Henna is made from the crushed leaves of the henna plant. It is a natural herbal blend and will even condition the skin. The smell is a combination of earth, clay, chalk, and damp green leaves. Henna colors come in crimson, burnt tobacco brown, and sunset russet. Although black is not a traditional henna color, many mehndi providers offer this color upon customer request.

Bridal body decorators create geometric motifs out of henna paste, turning an ordinary pair of hands or feet into bejeweled slippers and gloves of sultry brocade. The palms, soles of feet, forearms, inner wrists, fingertips and the top of hands and feet are typically the areas that are decorated.

Henna Painting—An Ancient Art

Mehndi, the ancient art of henna painting, has been practiced for five thousand years throughout several countries in Africa, such as: Morocco, Algeria, Libya, Egypt, Mali, Niger, Sudan, Senegal, and Ethiopia.

The application process can take anywhere from ½ hour to one hour depending on the design; and it may last anywhere between one week to one month depending on the area to which it is applied and how much that area is exposed to water, soap, rubbing or chemicals. I recommend henna painting one or two days before the ceremony, so that it looks fresh. You may wish to try the process several months before the wedding to see if you are comfortable with it.

The Therez Fleetwood Bridal Collection offers several styles that can be beautifully enhanced by the art of Mehndi. Once you have selected your Afrocentric wedding style, you can determine if henna painting would complement your overall look.

Chapter 18
Completing The Look

Accessories are the finishing touches to your wedding ensemble. They are the accent pieces to your wedding dress, that help you complete your look. Jewelry, shoes, foundation garments, flowers, gloves, handbags, garters and money bags, are all accessories that will enhance your Afrocentric wedding ensemble.

Accessories are one of the best ways to solve the wedding dilemma of what to do about something old (perhaps your Grandmother's gemstone earrings), something new (get a "new" handkerchief from your maid of honor), something borrowed (maybe a best girlfriend's silver or gold bracelet) and something blue (try a sky-blue garter). Although this is a European tradition, African-American brides still like to incorporate this custom into their Afrocentric wedding attire. And, they are all accent pieces to your wedding dress and complete your look.

Don't wear an elaborate headpiece, hairdo or veil with too much jewelry. An elaborate necklace, bracelet and earrings can be cumbersome and can clutter the overall effect.

Jewelry

In many parts of Africa, the elaborate body decorations and jewelry worn at the wedding ceremonies reflect the importance of the occasion. A woman's most exotic and valuable jewelry is brought out at the time of her wedding; and often plays a more important role in the bride's attire, than the dress itself.

Selecting the right jewelry to complement your look is not an easy task. Whether it has sentimental value or was a cherished gift, the jewelry you plan to wear on your wedding day, should be special in some way.

Exotic Extras

Foot jewelry such as toe rings or an anklet can be worn if you are going down the aisle barefoot. Or, if you are wearing a strapless dress, you might opt to wear armbands to complete your look.

Earrings can be the perfect touch to complete your final Afrocentric look. You should select your earrings with your hairstyle and headpiece in mind and try them on prior to your wedding day. The best choices are sparkling diamonds or colorful stones, either hanging delicately or in studs. The rule of thumb is…the larger the headpiece, the smaller the earring.

The size of your jewelry should depend on the intricacy of your dress. If your gown and headpiece are ornate, choose jewelry that is simple and tasteful. However, if your gown and headpiece are simple and conservative, then your jewelry can be bolder and more stylish.

Remember, your wedding gown should be the centerpiece of attention. If your wedding gown is made out of African fabric or adorned with ethnic trims, then thin, delicate necklaces and matching earrings will nicely enhance your overall look. By keeping your look simple and your accessories to a minimum, you won't be over-accessorized; and the effect will be much more glamorous and sophisticated.

On the other hand, if you choose to wear a simple wedding dress and want to add an Afrocentric touch to your overall look, this can be done quite effectively with the right choice of jewelry. A fine bead necklace or beadwork piece imparts a spiritual energy.

Or, you may want to add larger pieces of jewelry made out of stones from Africa, a multi-layered beaded necklace, amber beads or large gold earrings.

Traditionally, in West Africa, a bride wraps her waist with numerous strands of beads, signifying her virginity. Waistbeads should primarily be worn under your wedding dress but, if you prefer, they can be sewn directly on the dress at the high hip to add color and sensuality. They are particularly beautiful when they're made in your wedding colors with pearls, and silver or gold trinkets. To draw further attention to the bride, waistbeads are often accompanied by sound effects, such as the rattling of cowrie shells; but even the sound that eclectic assemblages of beads produce are intended for the ears as well as the eyes.

Here are some helpful hints to help you select the right jewelry to bring out the best in your face shape.

- ✸ Rounded or soft-edged jewelry pieces complement sharp, squared facial features. Wear circular chokers and rounded shapes at your throat to help soften a square jawline. Choose oval and round earrings and pins.

✳ Jewelry that adds length will be most flattering to your round face. Wear angular or geometric (square or diamond) shapes that cause the eye to move vertically. Angular-shaped dangle earrings and necklaces that end in a "V" are great selections.

✳ Horizontal shaped jewelry will add width to your oblong face shape. Wearing circular, crescent or swirl-shaped earrings will add width by making your eyes more horizontal. Choose short necklaces or chokers to reduce the length of your face. Select beads that are round or oval.

✳ Choices for your perfect oval face type are wide open! You can wear all lengths, widths and shapes of necklaces and earrings.

Which facial shape are you? Square, round, oblong or oval?

Square	Your face has straight, angular lines and the forehead is squared. The cheekbones and jawline are the same width and a square jaw is the dominant feature.
Round	Your face is as wide as it is long, with a soft rounded jawline and short chin. The hairline is also rounded.
Oblong	Your face is the same width at your forehead, cheekbones and chin. Your chin is angular and your jawline is narrow. Your temple area is shallow and your forehead is high.
Oval	Your face is balanced, with some prominence in the cheekbone area.

Gloves

Gloves are not typically worn with Afrocentric attire. However, if you choose to wear them, depending on your outfit, (either a contemporary ballgown or A-line) there are varying fabrications and lengths and to choose from. If your wedding dress has no sleeves or short sleeves, you may decide to wear long gloves. With three-quarter length sleeves, you may prefer to wear short gloves. If you do decide to wear gloves, be sure to match the color.

Handbags

Handbags should be small and used for necessities only. Usually your maid-of-honor is responsible for holding your cosmetics and other personal items throughout the reception. However, if you plan to carry a handbag, look for interesting shapes and details that coordinate with your gown and shoes. When choosing the shape of your handbag, consider your dress and the formality of your wedding.

Money Bag

A money bag is a small fabric bag made especially to hold envelopes and cash. You might wish to have your money bag made or trimmed with Afrocentric fabric or beads that match your wedding gown.

Handkerchief

A lace handkerchief is traditional; or hand-batiked silk could make an exquisite alternative.

Bridal Garter

A bridal garter is worn if you plan to honor the tradition of tossing the garter. It is often blue and can be decorated with ribbon, rosettes, lace and even tiny pearls, beads and shells. They are also nice with an ethnic flavor like cowrie shells sewn into them or a crocheted version that incorporates pieces of African fabric.

Chapter 19
Underneath It All

Foundation Garments

What you wear underneath your gown should be as glamorous as your wedding dress. Beautiful bras, slips, bustiers and petticoats do more than make you feel elegant. These items are most crucial to the proper fit and comfort of your wedding gown. If chosen wisely, they will enhance your figure and improve the fit of your dress.

Before you go shopping, ask your wedding consultant or designer to suggest the proper undergarments that will give you the best support for your specific Afrocentric wedding dress. I recommend that you try on your lingerie before you buy it to make sure it is not constricting and does not pinch. It should fit well and be comfortable and supportive; and it should never show through your gown.

Always select finely constructed undergarments, because ill-fitting ones will detract from even the most beautiful dress. Have a salesperson help you obtain the proper fit. Try on several styles until you find the right one for you.

> You should be just as diligent about finding that perfect piece of lingerie as you are about finding the perfect wedding dress.

117

Undergarment colors are a matter of opinion. Some designers will suggest that you purchase undergarments that are similar in color to your wedding gown. Others believe that you should wear hues that match your skin tone. I feel that each situation is unique. The best way to tell which color works best is to try both shades on with your wedding gown.

It's not easy to smooth out certain curves or create cleavage; however, there are several body shapers on the market that will flatter and enhance your figure. They will nip your waist, lift your butt and flatten your tummy—what more could you ask for!

Wearing sexy lingerie makes you feel good about yourself; and it is the one thing that never goes out of style. Good lingerie is an investment that you can wear again for many years, long after you've placed your wedding gown in storage.

Your First Fitting

You should have suitable undergarments purchased by the time of your first fitting. Make sure you go to all your fittings with the appropriate items.

The Bare Necessities

Bras

The proper bra can define and emphasize your bust or minimize it. When buying a bra, the cup should completely surround the breast, (with the exception of a push-up bra.) If there are bulges at the top or the sides of the bra, then this means that the bra cups are too small. Also, the bra shouldn't ride up in the back; if it does, the bra is probably too large.

There are a variety of bra styles available, such as: under-wire, demi cup, push up and cleavage enhancing. If you're wearing a strapless or an off-the shoulder wedding dress, you'll need a strapless bra; and a sheer-back dress, of course requires a low-back bra. For a perfect finish, be sure to choose the bra that works with the fabric of your Afrocentric wedding dress (if your fabric is clingy, avoid lace—the bra pattern will show through).

Bustier

A bustier is a long style bra, which fits to the waist, designed for strapless, off-the-shoulder and low back dresses. It is usually constructed with boning and push-up cups.

Best Bets

Halter gowns	A bra with convertible straps that can be worn many ways or a halter strap bodysuit.
Strapless gowns	Strapless bras or strapless corseted bodysuits.
Backless gown	Backless bustier.
Sheath	A seamless body suit or a seamless slip.

Panties   Look for seamless panties to pull you together and create structure, particularly if you are wearing soft, flowing fabrics.

Corsets   Corsets were worn for centuries by women who wanted to narrow their waists. They are more structured pieces with old fashion stays, boning, and waist cinchers. These are good to wear with stiffer, more tailored fabrics.

Garters   Garters are decorative elastic bands worn under your wedding dress usually placed mid-thigh. However, they are only appropriate for certain bridal gown silhouettes, such as the Ballgown or A-line styles. Under a sheer, revealing or form-fitted gown, garters can look quite bulky.

Garter Belt   A garter belt is a woman's undergarment for keeping her stockings up (similar to suspenders). It is very feminine and, for many brides, might be a perfect way to hold up your stockings. A garter belt is not recommended for a sheath or form-fitting gown, as it might show through.

Petticoats   The right petticoat can improve the shape and movement of your wedding gown. Most ballgowns and some A-line styles require that you wear a petticoat or hoop skirt. Petticoats (usually made of tulle or stiff netting, with high or low waists) come in various degrees of fullness. Choose a very layered petticoat for lots of fullness, a not-so layered one for a less full skirt. Hoops work best with the fullest of skirts. These are circular nylon slips with horsetail boning worn underneath your dress to give it shape. A slim sheath needs a body-clinging liner with a side slit. Ask your designer where you might find the appropriate slip or petticoat.

Wedding Day Stockings

When it comes to your wedding day stockings, look for interesting textures. Fishnet, lacy or floral patterns, ankle or side embroidery. Another option is satiny, glimmering fabric. For an ultra-sexy look, forgo pantyhose altogether and choose thigh high stockings with a lacy top.

Stockings

Sheer stockings held up by garters or ones that stay up by themselves look great under your wedding gown. You'll find stockings, thigh-highs and panty-hose in an array of colors, textures and patterns. When purchasing hosiery, try to take a swatch of your dress to match the hue correctly, because not all whites are alike. I suggest to always have a second pair on hand for your wedding day just in case they rip or snag.

Chapter 20
Putting Your Best Foot Forward

Choosing your Shoes

Finding the right shoes for your Afrocentric wedding may be just as exciting as choosing your gown. Whether you choose to go the traditional route with shoes that match perfectly, or opt for more creative alternatives, it is important to give thought to the many footwear possibilities for your wedding day. Sometimes it takes a bit of searching and investigating to find the perfect shoes, but it's well worth the trouble.

Keep in mind that your shoes should complement your dress. The great thing is you are no longer limited in your selection. Look for shoes that have a nice balance with your dress in design and structure. There are a variety of beautiful styles that you can wear again long after your wedding; so, you don't have to spend a fortune on shoes that you may never wear again. There are inexpensive styles in fabrics like silk-satin or crepe that can look as chic as costly pairs.

As a bride, you should never underestimate the importance of your wedding shoes. They are a significant accessory for your wedding, so you must give as much thought to your shoes as you do to any of your other bridal accoutrements.

Since you can't lug your wedding gown around from store to store when shoe shopping, you should carry a Polaroid of your dress and fabric swatches to make sure your shoes match your dress as closely as possible. Also, make sure you've purchased you shoes in time for your fittings so that your dress can be hemmed at the right length.

Unless you are used to wearing high heels, they are not always practical as a wedding shoe. You'll be on your feet a long time, from the ceremony through the reception line and dancing afterward, so you'll need shoes that offer fashion and comfort in equal parts.

If you are getting married outdoors where you'll be walking across uneven paths and across a lawn or field, then look for shoes with a wider heel than you might normally select. A wide heel or delicate flat will give you stability whereas a stiletto-thin heel will catch the ground like cleats.

If you are getting married on the beach, a low heel or fitted sandal is the best to keep the sand from irritating you feet and will keep you steady on uneven walkways and soft patches of earth.

Shopping Tip

Shop for shoes in the afternoon, when feet are likely to be largest (feet swell during the day).

Styles That Flatter

If your Afrocentric wedding dress is toned down and simple, you may opt for a more stylish shoe; as opposed to a more elaborate ensemble, whereas your shoe should be simpler and more toned down.

You'll want to choose a style that flatters your legs and complements your gown—high heels, sling backs or mules for a short dress or sophisticated sheath, mid-heel pumps or flats for a floor-length gown.

Although many brides wear pumps, you're not limited to this style. During warm-weather months you can wear a strappy, open shoe, with a simple, sexier dress or sheath. During the colder months, pumps, closed-toe sling backs, mules and even delicate boots can be worn.

The time of year you are getting married will determine the material and the type of shoe you choose whether it is fabric or leather, closed-toe, pump or sandal. Most bridal shoes are made in satin; however, leather and other materials work just as well. You'll find beautiful fabrics (satin, silk, moiré, faille, brocade) in a variety of styles and heel heights (flats, pumps, sling backs and sandals). If you are going to have ornamentation's of any sort such as cowrie shells, pearls, embroidery, or lace, make sure they do not overpower your dress.

You can also be creative with inexpensive dye-to-match shoes. With a hot glue gun and different trims, you can be very creative—adding subtle, personal flair to an old standard. If you have cowrie shells on your dress, you may want cowrie shell on your shoes.

Contour Your Feet

If you have wide feet, and want to make your foot look slimmer, choose shoes that cover part of the heel and part of the toe, and try an ankle strap to draw eyes away from the widest part of your foot.

Comfort, of Course

Remember, comfort is your priority. When buying your wedding shoes, you'll want to consider the heel height, the size and the material. The heel height you choose should be determined by the look of your wedding dress and the location of your wedding. If you are getting married outdoors the width of your heel will be thicker then what you would wear indoors.

If you are someone who doesn't regularly wear high heels and has difficulty walking in them, you might want to find a beautiful low, or flat slipper rather then a high-heeled shoe.

Another option is to have two different pairs of shoes. If you prefer to wear heels during the ceremony, get a higher pair to walk down the aisle in and a lower pair for dancing at the reception. It's not unusual to tuck flat shoes underneath the chair at the reception just in case your feet begin to ache. They're perfect for dancing.

If you are concerned about the discomfort of new shoes, you may want to practice walking in them in order to break them in so that you get used to their feel. (But take precautions to avoid soiling them.) Or, you may want to buy them a half size larger to avoid having to stretch them out.

What Color Is Your Rainbow?

Nowadays there are so many options that you can consider when buying your wedding shoes. It's not always necessary to choose basic white satin, inexpensive, dyed-to-match pumps. If you want to stray from standard bridal shoes, make sure you find shoes that match your dress perfectly whether they are white, bone, silver, gold or any other color in fabric or leather.

If you are wearing white or ivory and choose to wear a pair of colored shoes for your wedding, a pale pastel or light metallic would be nice. Just make sure you pick this same color up in other accessories as well.

You could also go with a very subtle tint of your wedding gown color. If you have a silver or gold accent on your dress, you might want to go with a silver or gold accent on your shoe. You may also choose a shoe to work with an accent color in your dress. However, it you select a color based off of trims or any other adornment on your dress, the shoe should be simple, soft, and subtle. The color should also match as closely to the color in you dress as possible.

Always take a swatch of fabric from your dress when shoe shopping no matter what style you choose. This will assure that the colors work together nicely.

Choose The Best Heel Height

Even if you have not chosen your ideal shoes for the wedding yet, make sure you wear the same heel height for your fittings as you will wear on your wedding day. This way the length of your dress can be determined correctly.

Chapter 21
Elaborate Extras: Flowers & Cakes

Flowers

Throughout the ages, flowers have been an enduring symbol of love, fertility and romance. They breath life and joy into any celebration and also provide splashes of color and a stunning natural backdrop for wedding photographs. They are the last accessory a bride picks up before she walks down the aisle.

The choice of your wedding bouquet depends on the style of your gown. Make sure your florist sees a photo of your gown. You don't want anything to cover or take away from the detail of your dress. Think tone and balance. They should work together. The bouquet size should be in proportion to the bride. A bouquet that is too large will simply overpower you and clutter your beautiful dress. Carry your bouquet as low as possible, pulling your shoulders back—this makes you look taller, thinner and more confident.

> Flowers lend fragrance and color, and define your wedding's unique personality.

Bouquets can create as much confusion for the bride-to-be as finding the perfect wedding dress. You should consult with your florist to provide information on the best bouquet for you. Here are some questions to ask when selecting your flowers:

❋ Should I use just one type of flower or a mixed arrangement?

❋ Should the bouquet be large or small?

❋ What color(s) should I use?

❋ What bouquet shape is most suitable and flattering to my wedding dress?

❋ Should there be a ribbon wrapped around my bouquet or a bow?

❋ How do bouquet shapes, sizes and flowers vary in price?

❋ What flowers will be in season on my wedding day?

❋ How will you assure that the flowers will not be wilted on my wedding day?

❋ What time, and where will the flowers be delivered?

For practical reasons, try to use flowers that are in season. To enhance the romance of the occasion, select fragrant flowers. Do not except wilted flowers or unopened buds from your florist; make sure your flowers are blooming for your big day.

Bouquets vary from the loose, fresh-picked-from-the garden look to the highly stylized formal cluster. Roses are the number-one choice of brides, followed by orchids. White flowers with a touch of greenery have traditionally been used for wedding bouquets. Whereas, more colorful flowers are often chosen to coordinate with the bridesmaid's attire or wedding colors. Your Afrocentric wedding, depending on your theme colors, will offer you more color options than your typical white floral arrangement. Don't be afraid to experiment.

Throwaway Bouquet

Talk to your florist about creating a "throwaway" bouquet for you to toss during the reception. Get the cost in writing.

Bridal Bouquet Shapes:

Cascade	A large, tear shaped arrangement in which flowers gracefully spill downward.
Nosegay	A tightly bound cluster of small flowers, round in shape.
Arm Bouquet	A graceful crescent shape designed to be cradled in one arm.
Biedermier	Concentric circles of flowers in different colors.
Hand-tied	A simple cluster of long stems, tied with a ribbon.
Spray	Usually a triangular shaped cluster of flowers.
Pomander	A ball of flowers suspended from the wrist by a decorative ribbon.

You might consider a deep red or purple bouquet for an evening wedding. It is more provocative with rich colors than with pastels. However, for daytime weddings, soft Pastels and rich golden yellows are perfect for daytime weddings.

Most brides order a bouquet, flowers for the bridesmaids and flower girl, boutonnieres for the groom and ushers, centerpieces for the reception, and corsages or boutonnieres for both sets of parents. If possible, you should order your flowers as early as six months before your wedding or shortly after you have ordered your wedding gown.

The honor attendant and the bridesmaids' bouquets are usually similar in shape to the bride's bouquet, but smaller and in harmony with the wedding colors. Usually, mother's and grandmothers of the bride and groom receive corsages or miniature floral wrist bouquets bands in colors that complement their dresses.

The boutonniere is a flower that the men traditionally wear on their left lapel. The groom wears a different flower from the ushers or his father to distinguish his role of honor. He often wears a flower found in his bride's bouquet. Popular choices for the boutonniere include the rose, carnation, freesia, or calla lily, bachelor's button or lily of the valley.

It's always nice to choose flowers that have significance to you and your groom as a couple. Perhaps he bought you yellow roses on your first date; or maybe you have a favorite color that can be tied into the wedding theme at this point. For your perfect Afrocentric wedding, don't be afraid to be creative and; be sure to find a florist who thinks like you.

Think Color For Your Perfect Afrocentric Wedding

Summer colors Look for blooms in citrus and coral colors like chartreuse, lavender, yellow, orange, peach, pink.

Fall colors For crisp autumn elegance, try greens and burgundies with a touch of white.

Spring colors Think pretty pastels like pink or peach—or pick purple for a bolder look.

Winter colors Think warmth by bundling together shades of red.

Artificial Flowers

Artificial flowers have come a long way since the days of garish, stiff petals and stems that look anything but natural. High-quality silk flowers and greens are now available that seem just picked from the garden. There are even scent crystal and pellets on the market that add whiffs of natural floral fragrance. You can blend silk or dried flowers with real one—they'll be a lasting keepsake. Also consider silk or dried flowers if you or your attendants have an allergy problem.

A Lasting Impression

Talk to your florist about preserving your bouquet for you or recommending someone who can.

Flowers and Their Meanings

Amaryllis	Pride	Lily of the Valley	Happiness
Apple Blossom	Hope, good fortune	Marigold	Affection
		Mimosa	Secret love
Azalea	First love	Myrtle	Love, remembrance
Beech	Prosperity		
Bellflower	Gratitude	Orange blossom	Purity
Bluebells	Consistency	Orchid	Rare beauty
Blue Periwinkle	Friendship	Pink Rose	Perfect happiness
Blue Violet	Modesty, faithfulness	Red & White Roses Together	Unity
Calla Lily	Beauty and elegance	Red Tulip	Declaration of love
Forget-Me-Not	True love		
Freesia	Innocence and trust	Stephanotis	Happiness and marriage
Gardenia	You are lovely	Violet	Faithfulness and virtue
Heliotrope	Devotion		
Ivy	Fidelity	White Rose	Only for thee, worthiness
Larkspur	Laughter	Yellow Tulip	Hopeless love
Lily	Majesty		

Reception Flowers

Like the music that's played and the food that's savored, your reception flowers can set a mood. Just like the flowers at the church, they should be color-coordinated with the hues of your wedding bouquet. They can turn a stark, non-descript room into a stunning can't forget one. For a different ambiance, you might even wish to dress your reception with Ficus trees, palms or other greenery that can be rented for the day.

Food Notes

Regardless of the type of meal you planning for your wedding reception, it is smart to take into consideration the eating habits of all the guests. There are sure to be some people who are non-meat eaters, or for health reasons can't eat sugar. It is a thoughtful gesture to have a special entrée and dessert available for you vegetarian guests, in addition to whatever else is set for the main course.

Your Wedding Cake—A Thing of Beauty

There's nothing like having your cake and eating it to. So, make sure you order a cake from a reputable baker, who is known for making succulent as well as fantastic-looking wedding cakes. Wedding cakes are thought of as a symbol of celebration and unity. Keep in mind that, next to you and your groom, your cake will probably be one of the most admired things at your wedding. Personal touches will make it especially memorable. By integrating different shapes, flavors, colors, frostings and decorative treatments, many couples are using their wedding cake to tell or remind their guests something about themselves. Once you have found your perfect baker, consult with him or her about your ideas and bring a photo of your wedding gown with you. Consider your Afrocentric theme and relay its importance to your baker, along with the shape, the size, the flavor, the filling and the icing of the cake.

Wedding Cake Advisory

- Start shopping for your cake about 3 months before the wedding.

- Ask to see photographs of cake samples.

- Taste the various flavors that the baker offers.

- Consider ordering an additional sheet cake with the same frosting (just in case).

- Ask the baker about delivery and set-up of the cake.

- Get everything in writing (cost, size, flavor, color, delivery date & time).

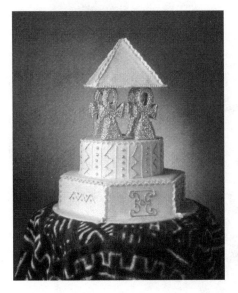

Cake decorations have evolved from the Caucasian bride and groom dolls, painted brown to represent African-Americans, to African-American brides and grooms dressed in traditional African garb. You may even prefer to forego the commercial images of a bride and groom; and instead top your cake with an Egyptian King and Queen or an Ankh. Other great options for your Afrocentric wedding cake would be to have your cake designed to match your wedding attire with adinkra symbols in ivory and gold, or, you might try a cake made in the shape of an African drum or mask, decorated in a mud-cloth print or trimmed in edible cowrie shells.

Chapter 22
The Bridal Party

Selecting Your Maid of Honor

Brides who have several close friends can be troubled over the selection of honor attendants. Your maid or matron of honor can be a younger or older sister, another relative or your best friend. If you are having a difficult time deciding which friend to ask, appoint a sibling or a close relative to this position. On rare occasions, some brides even ask a male friend or relative to serve in this role; he is then called a man of honor or honor attendant. In any event, the person that you choose should be an organizer, a good listener, and someone fun to be around because he or she will have the most responsibilities.

Selecting Your Bridesmaids

Bridesmaids play a prominent role on your special day; therefore, you should choose them carefully. The bridesmaids that you select can be those whom are closest to you, and not necessarily the ones you've known the longest. The number of attendants you have will depend on the size and tone of your wedding.

A small informal gathering may call for just one bridesmaid, while a large formal wedding could have up to a dozen bridesmaids.

When selecting your wedding party, first decide how many bridesmaids you want. You can select from relatives, friends and your fiancé's family, choosing those who reflect just what you have envisioned for you big day. Make sure that you select women who are supportive of your decisions, enthusiastic, encouraging and dependable.

Usually bridesmaids purchase their own gowns and the bride provides the accessories.

Inform your bridal party in advance of the expected price range of their dresses so that those who cannot afford to participate can be asked to help in other areas of your wedding planning. Women who seem to be undecided or skeptical about participating can cause problems and should be dropped from your list.

Your bridesmaids will want to feel important so allow them to take on different tasks, from organizing party activities, to toasting at the reception, to lighting candles and even stuffing envelopes.

What Are My Options? Who Do I Choose?

* Although it is not required, it is a good gesture to invite at least one of the groom's sisters to be a bridesmaid.

* Sisters and sisters-in-law are all relatives, so by choosing family only you won't be offending anyone.

* Include a combination of friends and family (as many as 12) this way everyone feels included.

* Have no bridesmaids, but only a witness.

Dressing Your Bridal Party

Unfortunately finding Afrocentric bridesmaids dresses is not as easy as going into a bridal salon and pulling them off the rack. I have seen wedding themes ruined because the brides-maids dress were not complimentary to the bride's attire.

You should start shopping for your bridesmaids' dresses right after you have chosen your gown. It is probably best to go it alone your first time out, so you can get a sense of what's out there; or just bring one bridesmaid or honor attendant to have her try on a few looks. Once you have narrowed down your search, you can then bring the other bridesmaids so they'll feel like they have a say in what's going on.

While it is an honor and a compliment to be invited to be a part of someone's wedding party, it is also a financial burden, a bit of work and a potential fashion nightmare. Some women even equate being asked to be in a wedding party to wearing an ugly, cumbersome, flamboyant dress; this doesn't have to be the case.

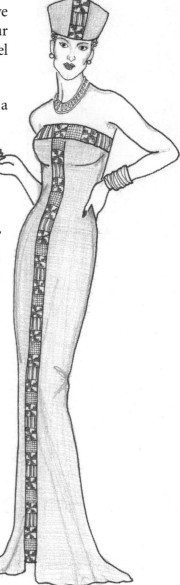

The best place to begin your search for your bridesmaids' gowns, is on the Internet. From the comfort of your home, you can browse through hundreds of styles and sort through them, based on price, style and designer. Although Afrocentric brides-maid's dresses are not the typical mainstream attire, this will give you an idea of the colors and styles that are out there. Even if you decide to have the gowns made, shopping around will make your mission easier, because you'll get some great ideas.

I often advise my clients to either:

❋ Buy standard bridesmaids' dresses from a local retailer and add ethnic trims to the dresses such as cowrie shells or African fabric.

❋ Buy simple dresses and fabulous ethnic jewelry with bold, colorful stones and trinkets to accent a sleek silhouette.

❋ Buy African fabric and have the dresses custom made.

With these options, each bridesmaid can choose a gown that suits her individual body and style best, without changing the look of your perfect wedding theme. Your bridesmaids can dress in a number of styles. A-line gowns, sheaths, two-piece ensembles, and empire-waist gowns are the best choices for most body types, as well as a traditional African design that can be worn in a wide range of colors, prints, and patterns.

Tradition dictates that the bridemaids' dresses should complement and coordinate well with the bride's gown. The easiest way to coordinate the bridesmaid's dresses with your style is to pick up on a single detail in your gown—a piece of trim, a hint of color, or the cut of the neckline—then search for bridesmaids' dresses with a similar style. The bridesmaids' dresses should never be longer than your wedding gown; and they should never be more elaborate.

It's always a good idea, however, to create a cohesive look throughout you wedding party and to conform the dress style of the bridal party to the dress style of the bride. For instance, if the bride is wearing a traditional, contemporary, alternative, or heirloom, then the bridal party should follow suit. When the bride's and her maids' attire blend and work well together, it always results in a beautifully styled wedding.

If you order your bridesmaids' dresses from a retailer, it is important that you refer to spec sheets for everyone's correct sizes. Your bridesmaids' measurements should be taken by a professional, over undergarments only (not over the clothing) with a tape measure that wraps around the body. Because women come in a variety of shapes and sizes, they must purchase their garments to fit the largest area of their body and tailor the smaller area to fit their specs. For example, if a woman's hips are a size 10 and her bust is a size 6, she should order her dress in the largest size, and then have the top altered to fit her smallest part.

How Do I Decide On the Color?

When choosing the color for your bridesmaids' dresses, you should ask yourself the following questions:

❀ What are my favorite colors?

❀ Which colors will most flatter the complexion(s) of my bridesmaids?

❀ Are the colors I'm considering appropriate to the time of day and degree of formality of the wedding?

❀ Will the colors lend themselves to appropriate ethnic traditions or theme weddings?

Pastels are the most widely used colors for daytime weddings in peach shades, champagne, even silver. Although they are standard and classic wedding colors, you don't have to rely on them. Challenge yourself and use unexpected colors for your bridesmaids.

These colors tend to work well on most African-American skin tones:

❀ Deep, rich, jeweled toned colors like emerald, ruby red, royal blue, fuchsia and orange.

❀ Darker colors like black, navy and **chocolate** have become acceptable as colors for attendants, for both daytime and evening weddings, because they can be worn again.

Although, your honor attendant's gown should be very similar in texture, style and color, she will have a little more flexibility with her choice because of her more distinguished role. You may choose to have her stand out in the crowd as the only one in your bridal party whose dress has a shawl; or have her carry different flowers from the rest of your attendants. She can even wear a different shade from what the other members of the bridal party are wearing.

- Charcoal is a trendy option for you wedding party since it has more richness and depth than black and is more acceptable to traditional parents and grandparents who don't think guests and attendants should wear black to a wedding.
- Soft pastels, silver, gold and earthy tones are nice.

You must also consider how the colors you choose will photograph. Use your own instincts and avoid shades that you feel are too vibrant. For example, lime green and vibrant red would not suitable colors for your attendants, because they tend to be so attention getting that they can take away from your center-stage star power.

The color of your bridal attendants' dresses can be selected as the single color statement of your wedding. Once you decide on a color for you bridal party, it adds a nice touch to carry this color scheme throughout the wedding decor, such as: in the flowers, trims, table linens, china, centerpieces, cake decorations, and even in the groomsmen's' accessories.

What Color Is Your Rainbow?

Color can be selected by the season or the time of day the wedding is being held:

Evening	royal blue, burgundy, black, navy
Sunset	orange, coral, red, gold
Afternoon	peach, purple and pastels
Autumn	sienna, moss, sage, chocolate, bronze, cranberry, cinnamon, hunter green
Summer	fuchsia, lavender

Keeping the Look Together

Finding Afrocentric bridesmaids' dresses is not an easy task. Since your bridesmaids will be a variety of diverse personalities with different opinions about the details of their dresses—from color, to fabric, to length—it is best that you shop for a style that you know the bridesmaids will be comfortable wearing for your perfect wedding day. The biggest challenge will be finding colors and garments that look good on more then one body type and various complexions.

You'll want to consider each bridesmaid's body shape individually and whether they'll be comfortable with their arms showing. Also determine whether they're extremely busty or flat-chested and whether they're uneasy about wearing a revealing dress. This way you can choose silhouettes that will flatter you each member of your bridal party's different shapes and sizes and incorporate culture into their attire. However, if you would like your bridesmaids' dresses to be made out of African fabric, unless you select traditional attire from Africa, you will probably have to find a good seamstress to work with.

All your bridesmaids should coordinate in many ways as possible. All elements of their ensembles should be considered from hair to nails to make-up colors to shoes. The trick is to pick something that suits each attendant perfectly and keeps her smiling all day. There are several options for selecting your bridesmaids' dresses. No rules says that all bridesmaids need to wear the exact same dress. The only guideline you should follow is to keep your wedding attendants visually cohesive, comfortable, and attractive; and be sure that you follow through with your Afrocentric theme on some aspect of their dresses.

1) Always start by selecting the color that you want your bridal party to wear. Then begin to think about the style of their dresses. If your bridesmaids come in a range of sizes, then you can make it easy on yourself by buying specific fabric(s) and

allowing each woman to have her own dress style made. This is a great idea if your best friends come in a variety of shapes and fashion personalities or if they live in different parts of the country. It is less stressful—and just as flattering—to let them pick distinct styles in the same colors and textures. A nice option is to choose three styles that complement different shapes and everyone will be happy; the gowns will fit their body types and the fabrics will work together harmoniously. Or, your bridal attendants can wear the same fabric and the same color but with different necklines and lengths that flatter each of them. To keep uniformity, they can wear identical jewelry, hairstyles and nail polish.

2) If you prefer not to vary your bridesmaids' attire, they can all wear the same Afrocentric style dress in different colors or in different shades of the same color, thus creating a beautiful spectrum of vibrant hues. However, you should find a style that will be flattering on your smallest bridesmaid to your largest bridesmaid. Styles that work well on sizes 4 through 24 are often sleeveless or ankle length dresses with A-line, princess-line or empire waist silhouettes. You can also allow your bridesmaids their own sense of individuality by allowing them to choose their own style of shoes and jewelry.

3) If your bridesmaids are wearing black, you can choose the length and fabric, then let them pick dress of their choice. This approach works best when you have a small bridal party, but will require a little more work for the bride. It is best that you accompany each bridesmaid when she shops for her dress to make sure that the various styles will all look harmonious together. If you are more flexible, and if you are having an informal ceremony, you can let your bridal attendants wear any kind of dress as long as it is a specific color.

What are the Best Silhouettes?
Bias cuts and A-lines are good silhouettes for most bridesmaids' dresses in sizes ranging from 4-18.

Things to keep in mind when choosing bridesmaid's attire:

- ❀ The maid or matron of honor may want to wear a different style or color.

- ❀ Dresses should be similar in line and degree of formality to your own. They may be the same length or shorter then yours; but all the hemlines should fall at the same place on each woman.

- ❀ Let your attendants know in advance if there are any special undergarments required to be worn under their dresses.

- ❀ Junior bridesmaids (aged 9 to 14) may wear outfits identical to those of other bridesmaids or, as an alternative, something more youthful.

- ❀ Flower girls may wear long or short dresses appropriate to the style of the wedding. Often they are in white with sashes or ribbons in wedding colors.

- ❀ After you have purchased your Afrocentric gown, then you can focus on the bridesmaids. Their gowns should compliment yours.

- ❀ If the bridesmaids are wearing dyable shoes, they should all be done at the same place, because dye lots can vary.

- ❀ Varying heights can be evened out by allowing each woman to wear a different heel height.

- ❀ The bridesmaids' jewelry and bouquets should be similar if not the same. The honor attendant's can be different.

- ❀ Headpieces and accessories, earrings, necklaces, gloves, hose and so on, should be the same for everyone.

The Mothers

The mothers of the bride and groom should choose outfits that complement the look of the bridesmaids. (Keep in mind how everyone will look standing next to each other).

Generally, the mother of the bride chooses her outfit first and then the bridegroom's mother selects something in a complimentary style and color. If one mom insists on a short dress and the other wants to wear a long dress, remind them of how lopsided it will look in the wedding album.

Child Attendants

❀ When choosing styles for children in the bridal party, keep their age in mind. Remember, they will run and play, even in wedding clothes.

❀ It is not necessary to dress your child attendants identical to your adult attendants. Junior bridesmaids certainly don't need to wear peek-a-boo backs; and little flower girls should wear ankle length skirts instead of floor lengths, which may cause them to trip.

❀ The flower girl's dress will often echo your Afrocentric bridal gown and can incorporate the same fabric, with a similar neckline and sleeves, as long as it doesn't look too mature.

❀ For a little diversity, you can also choose colors for the children that are complementary instead of exactly the same as the colors your adult attendants wear.

❀ For children, comfort is key; avoid scratchy fabric or headpieces that pinch; and make sure that when they try on their dresses, you should ask them how they feel; and don't neglect to have them walk in their shoes to stretch them out a little.

Chapter 23
Grooming Your Groom

On your wedding day, there is so much attention given to the bride. You are the centerpiece, but let's face it; your groom should look just as handsome as you will look beautiful. Even though the groom may not want to call as much attention to himself, the way he looks on his wedding day is still of the utmost importance. A groom can look very dashing, particularly if he has chosen the appropriate attire.

More and more men today take an active role in planning their wedding; and this includes what they will be wearing. Once you and your groom have decided on the theme and the formality of your Afrocentric wedding, and after you have chosen the style of your wedding gown, he should begin to coordinate his look.

You should allow your groom to select his own wedding attire, but you might want to participate in the process. This way you can make sure that the style he chooses will coordinate best with your overall look. The most important thing is that his outfit coordinates with yours and fits him correctly. A nicely fashioned groom should complement his bride's styling with a well-groomed image that completes the wedding picture.

Where Should He Shop for the Best Styles?

It's best to visit a men's formal wear store so that you and your groom can appreciate the range of choices and determine what works best for your celebration. Bring along magazine pictures of men's formal wear that you both like, swatches of your colors and your attendants gowns, and anything else regarding your ceremony and reception that might be helpful in selecting the right look.

Although the tuxedo is the most standard clothing choice, other suits may be preferable. Your groom can wear anything from a traditional bubah, a contemporary suit, or a shirt, slacks (pants) and waistcoat, or he can opt to wear a more informal look, which might include a tunic shirt with a Nehru collar, matching pants, and a band of aso-oke or kente fabric draped around his neck.

You and your groom should determine, given your bridal attire and that of your bridesmaids, whether the men in the wedding party would be more appropriately dressed in traditional African attire or contemporary styled attire.

Should He Buy or Rent His Tuxedo?

Your groom can choose to rent formal wear and use Afrocentric accessories such as a bow tie, cummerbund, ascot, vest and/or cuff links. I suggest having your accessories custom-made in either African print fabrics or the same fabric from your wedding dress. This way the wedding will look more uniform.

What Type of Wedding Are You Planning?

Depending on the time of year, the time of day, and the day of the week on which you're getting married, your groom has a number of styling options. If you are planning to have a contemporary styled wedding, he may choose to wear a tuxedo.

An alternative Afrocentric style wedding would call for a suit; or maybe you've decided on a traditional wedding with a complete African ensemble.

Contemporary

A formal wedding requires a tuxedo. Depending on the degree of formality and the time of day, the tuxedo might have tails, or it might not. Your groom might also need to know whether his jacket should be single or double-breasted; have shawl, peaked or notched collars; worn with bow ties versus ascots, versus neckties; and whether to wear a vest or cummerbund. Above all, style and comfort should be important issues to consider when selecting (the) formal attire.

For an avant-garde effect, a collarless tuxedo or one with a Nehru collar are great choices. Your groom might even opt to have his tuxedo custom made, replacing the satin lapels and the stripes on the legs and sleeves, with a silver, black or gold and black rabal cloth fabric from West Africa.

If the wedding is in the daytime and less formal, your groom might choose to wear a business suit. If you are getting married in a warm climate, he may opt to wear a more relaxed cream or white suit. In these cases, his tie can mirror the wedding party theme colors. All of these looks are elegant and sophisticated, so it's really a matter of what works best with your Afrocentric wedding theme and what style suits your groom's body type best.

Alternative

Alternative Afrocentric weddings are more casual and relaxed than contemporary Afrocentric weddings. They can be held any time of the day in a small or large ceremony.

Your groom can choose to wear a formal suit in his choice of colors and styles, with matching or contrasting trousers, a white or colored shirt and a great tie or ascot.

Other options are a light color dinner jacket with dark trousers; a 3/4-length mandarin jacket with matching pants; or shirt and vest in dark colors such as, black, gray, navy with slight African accents

He can also choose a more relaxed look in a white or cream colored linen drawstring pants, tunic shirt and vest accented with embroidery.

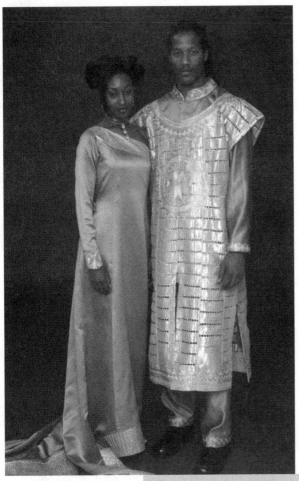

What Are His Options If He Doesn't Want to Wear a Tuxedo?

❀ For an informal wedding, the groom can dress in a modern suit and wear an African print tie or ascot.

❀ The groom may want to have his suit custom made to match the bride's fabric or have his vest, bow tie and cummerbund made out of one of the fabrics of her dress.

❀ If the bride is wearing traditional African fabric in aso-oke cloth, the groom may opt to have his suit Jacket made of the same fabric. The entire suit in aso-oke cloth would be too flashy unless it is a traditional bubah style as worn in West Africa. You might select interesting fabrics like kente cloth, brocades or other textures and ethnic prints.

Traditional

Traditional African styles consist of bubas made from kente cloth, guinea brocade or aso-oke. The silhouettes usually consist of four pieces; pants, top, tunic and hat. Each country has its own individual style. They are as follows:

Ghanaian	Batakali or Buruba—kente wrap over trousers and top in white lace or velvet.
Senegalese	Ngett Abdou or Grand Bubah—long embroidered tunic over pants made of aso-oke, guinea brocade or any royal fabric.
Ivorian (Ivory Coast)	Kente cloth bubah with crown.
Nigerian	Agbada—four-piece garment with pants, tunic top and soft hat.

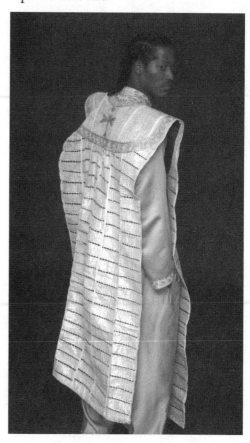

The Fit and Feel of Your Groom's Garments

The Jacket

Make sure your jacket is a perfect fit. It should be designed to fit your groom with clean lines and ease of movement.

1. When your groom's arms are held down at his sides, the hem of his coat should reach the curl of his fingers.

2. The sleeves should allow an inch of the shirt cuff to show.

3. The jacket should allow free movement of the arms; and the armholes shouldn't be snug.

4. The jacket should also fall smoothly across the groom's back; and when the arms move forward, the jacket shouldn't bundle up at the shoulders.

5. A man with narrow shoulders needs extra padding; and a slightly wider lapel can create the look of a fuller build.

6. A man with broad shoulders should wear a jacket with a shawl collar and slightly sloping shoulder pads to downplay their size.

There are various types of jackets that can be worn to complement your Afrocentric wedding gown. Help your groom to choose carefully for your perfect wedding style.

Jacket Styles

Cutaway coat (contemporary)

This coat is short in the front, long in he back, tapering from the front waist button to a wide back tail. Usually worn for formal day-time weddings.

Dinner Jacket (contemporary)

This is a snazzy alternative to the tuxedo. It is a white, ivory, or novelty-patterned jacket cut like a tuxedo jacket and worn with formal black trousers. Can be worn for both a formal and semi formal wedding.

Mandarin or Nehru Jacket (contemporary or alternative)

Has a standup collar and no lapels. This jacket buttons down the center front and usually worn with a mandarin-collared shirt.

Tuxedo Jacket (contemporary)

Worn for formal weddings when the reception starts after six p.m. The black or gray jacket may be single or double-breasted, with shawl, peak, or notch lapels in satin or grosgrain. It is worn with matching formal trousers, a bow tie, and vest or cummerbund.

Suit Jackets (alternative)

There are suit jackets that can be worn to flatter your groom's height and build. Just make sure he chooses one that enhances his silhouette, as well.

* A peaked lapel is a broad shape that points upward in a wide V at the collar.

* A notched lapel has a triangular indentation where it meets the collar.

* A shawl collar is a smooth, rounded lapel with no notch.

¾ Length Jackets (alternative)

This could include longer, tailored jackets falling 3" above the knee. Usually it is single breasted with various collar, pocket and sleeve treatments.

Shirts

❋ If your groom is wearing a tuxedo or dinner jacket, white is the best choice in 100% cotton fabric. Shirts with flat, sewn-down pleats look great with a tuxedo. The collar style should complement the lapel shape of the jacket; and if you are wearing a bow tie then a stiff short-to-medium-length collar, or wing tip is nice.

❋ Wing tipped collars are popular for formal weddings. However, they really don't fit in with the design direction for Afrocentric attire. This type of shirt is best worn with an evening suit or a formal tailcoat. It looks good worn with a bow tie or cravat (necktie).

❋ The most contemporary style of collar is the band collar, or Nehru collar. This style stands up around the neck and buttons at the man's throat.

❋ The lay-down collar is similar to a man's button-front shirt, but it folds over and around the neck. A wide space exists between the points in the front of the shirt. This is the most popular collar shape and is suitable for most jacket styles.

❋ Button down collar shirt—this is best worn with a simple plain suit, but you can jazz it up with an embroidered waistcoat (vest).

Pants

When hemming pants, the legs should be hemmed so they barely crease, while resting on the top of your groom's shoes.

Collars, Cuts & Cuffs

Double Breasted	Two rows of buttons run vertically down the jacket to close it.
Single Breasted	One strip of buttons runs vertically down the jacket to close it.
French Cuffs	Rollback shirt cuffs fastened with cuff links.
Laydown Collar	A turned-down collar, similar to business shirt collar, but in a formal fabric.
Notched Lapel	A lapel with a triangular cut, pointing inward.
Peaked Lapel	A lapel with a cut pointing upward.
Shawl	The lapel is uninterrupted by cuts; instead it is rounded.
Winged Collar	A formal dress shirt that sports a stand-up collar with folded down tips.

Groom's Checklist

- Make sure the clothes you are wearing are adequately pressed and hung somewhere safe.
- Try on your entire outfit one week before the wedding, making sure your pants are correctly hemmed, and your jacket is comfortable.
- Schedule your hair cut one week in advance.
- Double-check all your accessories and necessities: vest, cufflinks, tie, shoes, socks, shirt, underwear, cologne, etc.

Accentuating Your Body Type

Short & Slim   Single-breasted jackets with a low button will lengthen the look of the body and wide peak lapels will balance the effect.

For a slimmer frame, choose pants with reverse double pleats. You can give the illusion of extra height by wearing a single-breasted jacket with the button placed low on the torso.

Short & Stocky   A jacket with a slim collar works best.

Fit the jacket so that the top button falls in line with the top of the waist. This lends to a leaner look.

Your groom should avoid broad shoulders on his jacket and choose a natural shoulder line.

His pants should be reversed double pleats, as this adds length to the leg.

Tall & Husky   Avoid narrow and dainty neckwear; a fuller frame can handle a more pronounced tie.

Choose a shawl collar jacket. Pants that are a fuller cut so that the leg is not so snug are the best style for your groom's body type.

Tall & Slim   There are several options for a man of this physique.

Slightly broader shoulders and buttons that lie above the waistline look dashing on a man of this proportion.

Both the jacket and pants should be tailored to his body's natural shape.

Taller men can wear just about any style of jacket well, especially a double-breasted jacket with a tapered waist.

Formal Wear Terms To Know

Accessories

Ascot	A scarf like tie looped under the chin; worn with a cut away coat.
Boutonniere	Flowers, which coordinate with the bride's bouquet, worn on the left lapel by men in the wedding party, including the fathers.
Cummerbund	A pleated waist coat (worn instead of a vest) usually matched to a bow tie.
Four-in-Hand Tie	A knotted tie, similar to a business tie, but in a more formal fabric.
Pocket Square	A small, dressy handkerchief worn in the upper jacket pocket.
Slip-ons	Plain dress shoes in black patent or smooth leather.
Socks	Black cotton socks look better and are always more comfortable to wear than those thin nylon socks. Make sure the socks he wears go up to his calves. He'll be crossing his legs and dancing and his socks are going to show.
Studs & Cuff Links	Formal shirt fasteners that look like buttons but are considered as jewelry.
Suspenders	Used to hold up the trousers when a cummerbund is worn.
Ties	Bow tie vs. a real tie.
White Tie	The most formal evening attire is a white tie and white piqué vest, worn over a winged-collar shirt, with a black tailcoat and matching trousers.

What Should the Male Attendants Wear?

You and your groom should discuss whether he wants to be distinguished from his male attendants, or prefers to have them in the same Afrocentric style combination.

The best man can echo the groom by wearing a matching waistcoat of batik, kente or other African fabrics.

Junior ushers (aged 9 to 14) should wear what the adult ushers wear. Ring bearers may even wear outfits that resemble or match the men's attire.

Chapter 24
Preserving and Cleaning Your Afrocentric Bridal Gown

With a little care, your Afrocentric bridal gown can remain a prized possession for many years.

Never store your gown in a plastic bag after wearing it because plastics decompose, giving off fumes that can cause rapid oxidation of the fabric. You'll want to wrap the gown in a clean, undyed, unsized, unbleached, cotton sheet right after taking it off. Take it to the dry cleaners within the first 30 days after wearing it (the sooner the better).

Professional care by a dry cleaner can prevent your gown from turning yellow, brittle or a faded mess of fibers.

Don't Store Your Gown On A Hanger

Forget the plastic bag and padded hanger. To look great years down the line, your dress needs serious tender loving care.

Preserve Your Wedding Gown

Your gown should be turned inside out to protect beading and embroidery, and, if possible, should be cleaned individually, not in combination with other gowns. Make sure any bust and shoulder pads are removed before the cleaning process.

If you have a stain on your gown, don't ignore it. The longer a stain sits on your dress, the less chance there is of removing it, thereby creating a risk to the fabric. Be sure to tell the drycleaner where the stain is and what caused it. Also, make sure you know the fiber content of the gown and the types of beading used. Your cleaner should be able to tell you the best cleaning process for your dress if he or she is knowledgeable; if not, then find someone who is.

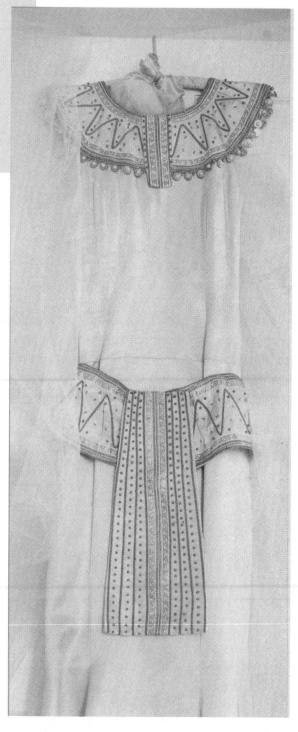

Store Your Headpiece Separately

Always store your headpiece separately. The glue, rubber and metal parts found in many headpieces can brown your dress over a period of time. For the same reason, don't store your gown with your shoulder pads.

Once your dress is cleaned, it should be wrapped in acid-free tissue paper, an all-cotton sheet, an unbleached cotton garment bag or a piece of freshly washed muslin; then boxed, never hung in an acid-free box (avoid plastic). Store the gown in a dry place away from heat and moisture, (not in the attic or basement) and it will last beyond your lifetime.

Conclusion

As an Afrocentric bridal gown designer, I feel such joy in seeing couples incorporating their heritage on one of the most important days of their lives, when African-American families join together in the union of love, honor and devotion. My designs entail mixing both heritages by incorporating the American philosophy of wedding planning and adding African elements.

In various countries throughout Africa, there is much delight in the preparation and the rituals that lead up to their wedding ceremonies, which may last anywhere from three days to one week. As African-Americans, however, most of us have grown up adapting to the American way of living. We've taken on the tradition of preparing for the "big day", but much of the emphasis for us has always been placed on the "look" of the wedding, from choosing our attire, the wedding cake, and the decorations for the reception hall.

With the realization that marriage is not just between the bride and groom, but between their families as well, a growing number of African-Americans, have made the decision to celebrate their union by reaching back and paying homage to their African ancestors. This is what makes us, as a people, so unique, not allowing our heritage to leave us; and by constantly finding ways to keep our tradition alive, through art, music and even our wedding ceremonies.

One of the rituals that has become popular at many African-American wedding ceremonies is "Jumping the Broom." The ritual, which is often practiced in accordance with the traditional American ceremonies, evolved in early 19th century America, when Africans were enslaved in this country and were forbidden to marry by their slave owners. They thought if slaves were to marry they would grow stronger in number and revolt. Since blacks were denied this right, they had to invent their own ways of matrimony, thus became the process of "jumping the broom," which showed a couple's commitment to each other and indicated stepping into married life. The broom also held spiritual significance by sweeping away evil spirits from a couple's path and honored and blessed their new life together.

Today, this significance still holds true for thousands of African-American couples. Along with jumping the broom, several other cultural practices are incorporated into wedding ceremonies today, including: the rituals performed, the music we play, the foods we eat, and the clothes we wear.

My hope is that you have enjoyed reading *The Afrocentric Bride—A Style Guide*. My blessing is that I hear from you. My prayer is that your marriage lasts a lifetime. May god bless you, yours, and all those that come from you.

Spiritually yours,
Therez Fleetwood

Contact Information

Author & Bridal Gown Designer

Therez Fleetwood
34 Park Avenue, Suite 1
Bloomfield, NJ 07003
(212) 714-8058
email: therezdesigns@aol.com
www.therezfleetwood.com

The Therez Fleetwood Bridal Collection features an extensive selection of Afrocentric styles, including: wedding gowns and dresses, jewelry, veils, crowns and shoes.

The Therez Fleetwood Bridal Collection now offers Afrocentric bridesmaids' gowns and dresses.

Special Thanks To:

Photographers:

Cover photo by Tar
email tarboy@nyc.rr.com
www.tarboy.net

Wayne "Zoom" Summerlin
www.waynesummerlin.com

John A. Mitchell
JAMOGRAFIX
(973)223-1021

Eric VonLockhart
(212)463-0450

Models:

Grege Morris
Dionne Hanson
Nicki Norris
Sharon Quinn

Veroy
Nina Shay
Etta Francios
Yogi

Guest Designers:

Franklin Rowe International
(212)967-8763
email roweorig@aol.com

Cassandra Bromfield
400 West 42nd Street, Studio 3C
New York, NY 10036
(212)502-5277
email: cabcomp@aol.com

Beauloni by Sherri Hobson-Greene
556A Macon Street
Brooklyn, NY 11233
(718)452-2920
email info@beauloni.com
www.beauloni.com

Nigerian Fabrics & Fashions
584 Myrtle Avenue
Brooklyn, NY 11205
(718)260-9416
email: NFF1@MSN.com
www.nigerianfabricsandfashions.com

Wedding Cake:

Isn't That Special—Outrageous Cakes
720 Monroe Street
Hoboken, NJ 07030
(201)216-0123 /(212)722-0678
www.cakediva.com
Contact: Charmaine Jones

Brides & Grooms

Monique & Rod Bowen
Betsy & Anthony Jackson
Robin & Darnell Day

Shannell & Sekou Kwantu
Leian & Jean-Pierre Welch

Index

ORDER FORM

WWW.AMBERBOOKS.COM

African-American Self Help and Career Books

Fax Orders: 480-283-0991   Postal Orders: Send Checks & Money Orders to:

Telephone Orders: 480-460-1660   Amber Books Publishing

Online Orders: E-mail: Amberbks@aol.com   1334 E. Chandler Blvd., Suite 5-D67

Phoenix, AZ 85048

_____ *The Afrocentric Bride: A Style Guide*

_____ *The African-American Woman's Guide to Great Sex, Happiness, & Marital Bliss*

_____ *Beautiful Black Hair: A Step-by-Step Instructional Guide*

_____ *How to Get Rich When You Ain't Got Nothing*

_____ *The African-American Job Seeker's Guide to Successful Employment*

_____ *The African-American Travel Guide*

_____ *Suge Knight: The Rise, Fall, and Rise of Death Row Records*

_____ *The African-American Teenagers Guide to Personal Growth, Health, Safety, Sex and Survival*

_____ *Get That Cutie in Commercials, Televisions, Films & Videos*

_____ *Wake Up and Smell the Dollars! Whose Inner City is This Anyway?*

_____ *How to Own and Operate Your Home Day Care Business Successfully Without Going Nuts!*

_____ *The African-American Woman's Guide to Successful Make-up and Skin Care*

_____ *How to Play the Sports Recruiting Game and Get an Athletic Scholarship:*
      The Handbook and Guide to Success for the African-American High School Student-Athlete

_____ *Is Modeling for You? The Handbook and Guide for the Young Aspiring Black Model*

Name:_____

Company Name:_____

Address:_____

City:_____State:_____Zip:_____

Telephone: (____) _____E-mail:_____

For Bulk Rates Call: **480-460-1660**   **ORDER NOW**

The Afrocentric Bride	$16.95	❏ Check ❏ Money Order ❏ Cashiers Check
Great Sex	$14.95	❏ Credit Card: ❏ MC ❏ Visa ❏ Amex ❏ Discover
Beautiful Black Hair	$16.95	CC#_____
How to Get Rich	$14.95	
Job Seeker's Guide	$14.95	Expiration Date:_____
Travel Guide	$14.95	
Suge Knight	$21.95	**Payable to:**
Teenagers Guide	$19.95	Amber Books
Cutie in Commercials	$16.95	1334 E. Chandler Blvd., Suite 5-D67
Wake Up & Smell the Dollars	$18.95	Phoenix, AZ 85048
Home Day Care	$12.95	
Successful Make-up	$14.95	**Shipping:** $5.00 per book. Allow 7 days for delivery.
Sports Recruiting:	$12.95	**Sales Tax:** Add 7.05% to books shipped to Arizona addresses.
Modeling:	$14.95	**Total enclosed: $_____**